Schöningh

EinFach
Englisch

J. B. Priestley

An Inspector Calls

Edited by
Hans Kröger

Series Editor:
Hans Kröger

Acknowledgements

Illustrations

cover: © stokkete – Fotolia.com; p. 4: two photos: Cinetext, Frankfurt; p. 4 centre left: © Featureflash/shutterstock.com; p. 4 centre: © Joe Seer/shutterstock.com; p. 4 bottom right: Archiv für Kunst und Geschichte, Berlin; p. 4 bottom left: © picture-alliance/dpa; p. 73, 75: © picture-alliance/dpa; p. 76–77: © Posy Simmonds 1989, taken from: The Guardian, April 1989

Film version

J. B. Priestley's *An Inspector Calls*. Directed by Guy Hamilton. Written for the screen by Desmond Davis. Lion Film, Watergate, 1954.

Sprachliche Betreuung: Susan Ashworth-Fiedler

www.schoeningh-schulbuch.de
Schöningh Verlag, Jühenplatz 1–3, 33098 Paderborn

Druck A 14 13 12 / Jahr 2017 16 15
Alle Drucke der Serie A sind im Unterricht parallel verwendbar.
Die letzte Zahl bezeichnet das Jahr dieses Druckes.

Umschlaggestaltung: Jennifer Kirchhof
Druck und Bindung: westermann druck GmbH, Braunschweig

ISBN 978-3-14-041200-1

Contents

Getting started

Which of these persons do you know? What is typical of them? What are they like? How do they differ from each other? Make some notes.

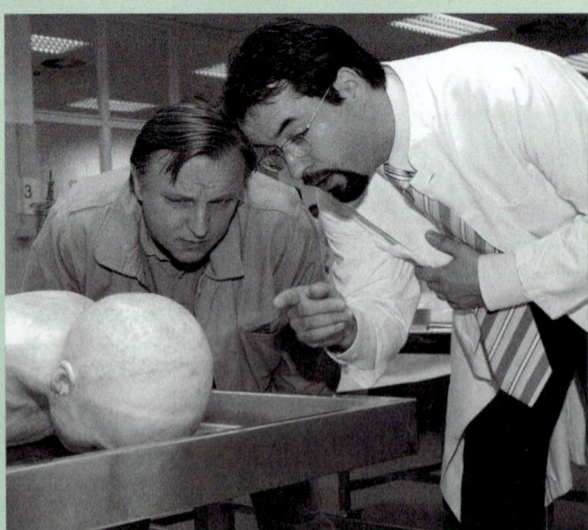

➤ Draw the cover for a new edition of *An Inspector Calls.*

➤ Write a letter to the publishing house in which you explain the advantages of your sketch to the publishing manager.

Characters

Arthur Birling ⚭ Sybil Birling

Sheila Birling ♥ Gerald Croft

Eric Birling

Edna

Inspector Goole

Acts

All three acts, which are continuous, take place in the dining-room of the Birlings' house in Brumley. It is an evening in spring, 1912.

Brumley is a fictitious name. It is a typical industrial city in the North Midlands – similar to Birmingham.

Act One

The dining-room of a fairly large suburban house, belonging to a prosperous manufacturer. It has good solid furniture of the period. The general effect is substantial and heavily comfortable, but not cosy and homelike. (If a realistic set is used, then it should be swung back, as it was in the Old Vic production at the New Theatre. By doing this, you can have the dining-table centre downstage during Act I, when it is needed there, and then, swinging back, can reveal the fireplace for Act II, and then for Act III can show a small table with telephone on it, downstage of fireplace; and by this time the dining-table and its chairs have moved well upstage. Producers who wish to avoid this tricky business, which involves two resettings of the scene and some very accurate adjustments of the extra flats necessary, would be well advised to dispense with an ordinary realistic set, if only because the dining-table becomes a nuisance. The lighting should be pink and intimate until the Inspector arrives, and then it should be brighter and harder.)

At rise of curtain, the four BIRLINGS *and* GERALD *are seated at the table, with* ARTHUR BIRLING *at one end, his wife at the other,* ERIC *downstage, and* SHEILA *and* GERALD *seated upstage.* EDNA*, the parlour-maid, is just clearing the table, which has no cloth, of dessert plates and champagne glasses, etc., and then replacing them with decanter of port, cigar box and cigarettes. Port glasses are already on the table. All five are in evening dress of the period, the men in tails and white ties, not dinner-jackets.* ARTHUR BIRLING *is a heavy-looking, rather portentous man in his middle fifties with fairly easy manners but rather provincial in his speech. His wife is about fifty, a rather cold woman and her husband's social superior.* SHEILA *is a pretty girl in her early twenties, very pleased with life and rather excited.* GERALD CROFT *is an attractive chap about thirty, rather too manly to be a dandy but very much the easy well-bred young man-about-town.* ERIC *is in his early twenties, not quite at ease, half shy, half*

✓ Mark words or lines that inform about characters and atmosphere (use different colours).

***suburban** outer area of a town or city
the period here: the years before World War I
substantial *vermögend*
***cosy** warm and comfortable
set here: stage scenery *(Bühnenbild)*
downstage at the front of the stage
centre downstage *Vordergrundmitte*
***to reveal** show
upstage at the back of the stage
producer *Regisseur*
flat here: *Kulisse*
to dispense with to do without
***nuisance** sth that causes trouble

parlour-maid *Dienstmädchen*

decanter *Karaffe*

tails (pl, coll) tail-coat *(Frack)*
portentous solemn, grave, causing respect by one's importance
***superior** *überlegen*
chap (infml) man
dandy man caring too much about clothes and appearance
well-bred showing good manners
man-about-town man who does not work, but spends time in clubs, theatres, etc.
***at ease** relaxed

assertive sharing a strong and confident personality

assertive. At the moment they have all had a good dinner, are celebrating a special occasion, and are pleased with themselves.

> **Stage directions** are added to inform the director of a play and the actors about the way in which the play should be performed. They also say what the characters and the stage should look like and where and when the action takes place.
> Stage directions also help the reader, who cannot see the play performed on stage, to get a vivid idea of what is going on.

governor (coll) one's father *('alter Herr')*
***pretend** give an appearance of
possessive here: enjoying possession
jolly (coll) very
y'know you know
***tray** *Tablett*

BIRLING: Giving us the port, Edna? That's right. *(He pushes it towards* ERIC.) You ought to like this port, Gerald. As a matter of fact, Finchley told me it's exactly the same port your father gets from him.

GERALD: Then it'll be all right. The governor prides himself on being a good judge of port. I don't pretend to know much about it.

SHEILA *(gaily, possessively)*: I should jolly well think not, Gerald. I'd hate you to know all about port – like one of these purple-faced old men.

BIRLING: Here, I'm not a purple-faced old man.

SHEILA: No, not yet. But then you don't know all about port – do you?

BIRLING *(noticing that his wife has not taken any)*: Now then, Sybil, you must take a little tonight. Special occasion, y'know, eh?

SHEILA: Yes, go on, Mummy. You must drink our health.

MRS. BIRLING *(smiling)*: Very well, then. Just a little, thank you. *(To* EDNA, *who is about to go, with tray.)* All right, Edna. I'll ring from the drawing-room when we want coffee. Probably in about half an hour.

EDNA *(going)*: Yes, ma'am.

EDNA *goes out. They now have all the glasses filled.*

BIRLING *beams at them and clearly relaxes.*

BIRLING: Well, well – this is very nice. Very nice. Good dinner too, Sybil. Tell cook from me.

GERALD *(politely)*: Absolutely first-class.

MRS BIRLING *(reproachfully)*: Arthur, you're not supposed to say such things –

BIRLING: Oh – come, come – I'm treating Gerald like one of the family. And I'm sure he won't object.

SHEILA *(with mock aggressiveness)*: Go on, Gerald – just you object!

GERALD *(smiling)*: Wouldn't dream of it. In fact, I insist upon being one of the family now. I've been trying long enough, haven't I? *(As she does not reply, with more insistence.)* Haven't I? You know I have.

MRS BIRLING *(smiling)*: Of course she does.

SHEILA *(half serious, half playful)*: Yes – except for all last summer, when you never came near me, and I wondered what had happened to you.

GERALD: And I've told you – I was awfully busy at the works all that time.

SHEILA *(same tone as before)*: Yes, that's what *you* say.

MRS BIRLING: Now, Sheila, don't tease him. When you're married you'll realise that men with important work to do sometimes have to spend nearly all their time and energy on their business. You'll have to get used to that, just as I had.

SHEILA: I don't believe I will. *(half playful, half serious, to* GERALD.) So you be careful.

GERALD: Oh – I will, I will

ERIC *suddenly guffaws. His parents look at him.*

SHEILA *(severely)*: Now – what's the joke?

ERIC: I don't know – really. Suddenly I felt I just had to laugh.

SHEILA: You're squiffy.

ERIC: I'm not.

MRS BIRLING: What an expression, Sheila! Really, the things you girls pick up these days!

ERIC: If you think that's the best she can do –

SHEILA: Don't be an ass, Eric.

MRS BIRLING: Now stop it, you two. Arthur, what about this famous toast of yours?

beam smile brightly

reproachful expressing blame ⁄ or criticism

you're not supposed to *so* ⁄ *etwas sagt man nicht*

mock pretending

works (pl) factory

⮜ What does Sheila's reaction show?

***to tease** to make fun of, provoke in a playful way

to guffaw [gʌ'fɔ:] to laugh loudly

squiffy (coll) slightly drunk

ass (infml) a stupid person

toast *Trinkspruch*

cable a telegraphed message

/ ***rude** impolite
have done with it get it finished

/ **frank** open, direct
without any pretences quite honestly
/ **tremendous** very much

Limited (of a company) having a limited liability
Ltd (abbr) *GmbH*

***to compete (with/against)**
competition
competitive / competitor

/ **fortunate** lucky
anyhow at least

BIRLING: Yes, of course. *(Clears his throat.)* Well, Gerald, I know you agreed that we should only have this quiet little family party. It's a pity Sir George and – er – Lady Croft can't be with us, but they're abroad and so it can't be helped. As I told you, they sent me a very nice cable – couldn't be nicer. I'm not sorry that we're celebrating quietly like this –

MRS BIRLING: Much nicer really.

GERALD: I agree.

BIRLING: So do I, but it makes speech-making more difficult –

ERIC *(not too rudely)*: Well, don't do any. We'll drink their health and have done with it.

BIRLING: No, we won't. It's one of the happiest nights of my life. And one day, I hope, Eric, when you've a daughter of your own, you'll understand why. Gerald, I'm going to tell you frankly, without any pretences, that your engagement to Sheila means a tremendous lot to me. She'll make you happy, and I'm sure you'll make her happy. You're just the kind of son-in-law I always wanted. Your father and I have been friendly rivals in business for some time now – though Crofts Limited are both older and bigger than Birling and Company – and now you've brought us together, and perhaps we may look forward to the time when Crofts and Birlings are no longer competing but are working together – for lower costs and higher prices.

GERALD: Hear, hear! And I think my father would agree to that.

MRS BIRLING: Now, Arthur, I don't think you ought to talk business on an occasion like this.

SHEILA: Neither do I. All wrong.

BIRLING: Quite so, I agree with you. I only mentioned it in passing. What I did want to say was – that Sheila's a lucky girl – and I think you're a pretty fortunate young man too, Gerald.

GERALD: I know I am – this once anyhow.

BIRLING *(raising his glass)*: So here's wishing the pair of you – the very best that life can bring. Gerald and Sheila.

MRS BIRLING *(raising her glass, smiling)*: Yes, Gerald, yes, Sheila darling. Our congratulations and very best wishes!

GERALD: Thank you.

MRS BIRLING: Eric!

ERIC *(rather noisily)*: All the best! She's got a nasty temper sometimes – but she's not bad really. Good old Sheila!

SHEILA: Chump! I can't drink to this, can I? When do I drink?

GERALD: You can drink to me.

SHEILA *(quiet and serious now)*: All right then. I drink to you, Gerald.

For a moment they look at each other.

GERALD *(quietly)*: Thank you. And I drink to you – and hope I can make you as happy as you deserve to be.

SHEILA *(trying to be light and easy)*: You be careful – or I'll start weeping.

GERALD *(smiling)*: Well, perhaps this will help to stop it. *(He produces a ring case.)*

SHEILA *(excited)*: Oh – Gerald – you've got it – is it the one you wanted me to have?

GERALD *(giving the case to her)*: Yes – the very one.

SHEILA *(taking out the ring)*: Oh – it's wonderful! Look – Mummy – isn't it a beauty? Oh – darling – *(She kisses* GERALD *hastily.)*

ERIC: Steady the Buffs!

SHEILA *(who has put ring on, admiringly)*: I think it's perfect. Now I really feel engaged.

MRS BIRLING: So you ought, darling. It's a lovely ring. Be careful with it.

SHEILA: Careful! I'll never let it go out of my sight for an instant.

MRS BIRLING *(smiling)*: Well, it came just at the right moment. That was clever of you, Gerald. Now, Arthur, if you've no more to say, I think Sheila and I had better go into the drawing-room and leave you men –

BIRLING *(rather heavily)*: I just want to say this. *(Noticing that* SHEILA *is still admiring her ring.)* Are you listening, Sheila? This concerns you too. And after all I don't often make speeches at you –

SHEILA: I'm sorry, Daddy. Actually I was listening.

She looks attentive, as they all do. He holds them for a moment before continuing.

*****nasty** bad, terrible /

chump (sl) a fool

beauty very beautiful engagement ring

Steady the Buffs! (sl) here: keep cool

*****actually** in fact /

*****attentive** taking careful notice

to hold to keep the attention of

BIRLING: I'm delighted about this engagement and I hope it won't be too long before you're married. And I want to say this: There's a good deal of silly talk about these days – but – and I speak as a hard-headed businessman, who has to take risks and knows what he's about – I say, you can ignore all this silly pessimistic talk. When you marry, you'll be marrying at a very good time. Yes, a very good time – and soon it'll be an even better time. Last month, just because the miners came out on strike, there's a lot of wild talk about possible labour trouble in the near future. Don't worry. We've passed the worst of it. We employers at last are coming together to see that your interests – and the interests of Capital – are properly protected. And we're in for a time of steadily increasing prosperity.

GERALD: I believe you're right, sir.

ERIC: What about war?

BIRLING: Glad you mentioned it, Eric. I'm coming to that. Just because the Kaiser makes a speech or two, or a few German officers have too much to drink and begin talking nonsense, you'll hear some people say that war's inevitable. And to that I say – fiddlesticks! The Germans don't want war. Nobody wants war, except some half-civilised folks in the Balkans. And why? There's too much at stake these days. Everything to lose and nothing to gain by war.

ERIC: Yes, I know – but still –

BIRLING: Just let me finish, Eric. You've a lot to learn yet. And I'm talking as a hard-headed, practical man of business. And I say there isn't a chance of war. The world's developing so fast that it'll make war impossible. Look at the progress we're making. In a year or two we'll have aeroplanes that will be able to go anywhere. And look at the way the automobile's making headway – bigger and faster all the time. And then ships. Why, a friend of mine went over this new liner last week – the *Titanic* – she sails next week – forty-six thousand eight hundred tons – New York in five days – and every luxury – and unsinkable, absolutely unsinkable. That's what you've got to keep your eye on, facts like that, progress like that – and not a few German officers talk-

hard-headed practical, realistic

labour trouble trouble caused by workers (e.g. strike)

to be in for to expect

the Kaiser: reference to the last German Emperor William II (1859–1941) who reigned from 1888 to 1918.

fiddlesticks! nonsense

/ **to be at stake** *auf dem Spiel stehen*

headway progress

liner a large passenger ship of a steamship company

Titanic: When she collided with an iceberg on her maiden voyage (April 14, 1912) nearly 1500 persons drowned.

ing nonsense and a few scaremongers here making a fuss about nothing. Now you three young people, just listen to this – and remember what I'm telling you now. In twenty or thirty years' time – let's say, in 1940 – you may be giving a little party like this – your son or daughter might be getting engaged – and I tell you by that time you'll be living in a world that'll have forgotten all these Capital versus Labour agitations and all these silly little war scares. There'll be peace and prosperity and rapid progress everywhere – except of course in Russia, which will always be behindhand, naturally.

MRS BIRLING: Arthur!

As MRS BIRLING *shows signs of interrupting*

BIRLING: Yes, my dear, I know – I'm talking too much. But you youngsters just remember what I said. We can't let these Bernard Shaws and H. G. Wellses do all the talking. We hard-headed practical businessmen must say something sometime. And we don't guess – we've had experience – and we know.

MRS BIRLING *(rising. The others rise)*: Yes, of course, dear. Well – don't keep Gerald in here too long. Eric – I want you a minute.

She and SHEILA *and* ERIC *go out.* BIRLING *and* GERALD *sit down again.*

BIRLING: Cigar?

GERALD: No, thanks. Can't really enjoy them.

BIRLING *(taking one himself)*: Ah, you don't know what you're missing. I like a good cigar. *(Indicating decanter.)* Help yourself.

GERALD: Thank you.

BIRLING *lights his cigar and* GERALD, *who has lit a cigarette, helps himself to port, then pushes decanter to* BIRLING.

BIRLING: Thanks. *(Confidentially.)* By the way, there's something I'd like to mention – in strict confidence – while we're by ourselves. I have an idea that your mother – Lady Croft – while she doesn't object to my girl – feels you might have done better for yourself socially –

scaremonger person who spreads reports intended to cause public fear *(Panikmacher/in)*

versus against ↗

G. B. Shaw (1856–1950), Irish dramatist, and **H. G. Wells** (1866–1946), English novelist. They both supported Socialism.

What is your view of the ideas presented by Mr Birling?

***confidential** *vertraulich* ↗

/ *__to embarrass__ to cause sb. to feel ashamed or socially uncomfortable
/ *__dissent__ disagreement, difference of opinion
__to check__ here: to stop
__county family__ a family of high social rank (noble) with a seat in the county (*vornehme Familie mit Ahnensitz in einer Grafschaft)*
__Honours List__ titles given to important people on the Queen's birthday and at New Year
__Lord Mayor__ *(Ober-)Bürgermeister*
__Royalty__ member of the royal family
__sound__ here: reliable, serious
__gather__ think, conclude
/ __knighthood__ *Ritterstand*
*__complacent__ self-satisfied
/ *__obstacle__ sth which stands in the way
__to tell stories__ to tell lies, funny anecdotes
__potty__ (coll) crazy, mad about

GERALD, *rather embarrassed, begins to murmur some dissent, but* BIRLING *checks him.*

No, Gerald, that's all right. Don't blame her. She comes from an old county family – landed people and so forth – and so it's only natural. But what I wanted to say is – there's a fair chance that I might find my way into the next Honours List. Just a knighthood, of course.

GERALD: Oh – I say – congratulations!

BIRLING: Thanks. But it's a bit too early for that. So don't say anything. But I've had a hint or two. You see, I was Lord Mayor here two years ago when Royalty visited us. And I've always been regarded as a sound useful party man. So – well – I gather there's a very good chance of a knighthood – so long as we behave ourselves, don't get into the police court or start a scandal – eh? *(Laughs complacently.)*

GERALD *(laughs)*: You seem to be a nice well-behaved family –

BIRLING: We think we are –

GERALD: So if that's the only obstacle, sir, I think you might as well accept my congratulations now.

BIRLING: No, no, I couldn't do that. And don't say anything yet.

GERALD: Not even to my mother? I know she'd be delighted.

BIRLING: Well, when she comes back, you might drop a hint to her. And you can promise her that we'll try to keep out of trouble during the next few months.

They both laugh. ERIC *enters.*

ERIC: What's the joke? Started telling stories?

BIRLING: No. Want another glass of port?

ERIC *(sitting down)*: Yes, please. *(Takes decanter and helps himself.)* Mother says we mustn't stay too long. But I don't think it matters. I left 'em talking about clothes again. You'd think a girl had never had any clothes before she gets married. Women are potty about 'em.

BIRLING: Yes, but you've got to remember, my boy, that clothes mean something quite different to a woman. Not just something to wear – and not only something to make 'em look prettier – but – well, a sort of sign or token of their self-respect.

GERALD: That's true.

ERIC *(eagerly)*: Yes, I remember – *(but he checks himself.)*

BIRLING: Well, what do you remember?

ERIC *(confused)*: Nothing.

BIRLING: Nothing?

GERALD *(amused)*: Sounds a bit fishy to me.

BIRLING *(taking it in same manner)*: Yes, you don't know what some of these boys get up to nowadays. More money to spend and time to spare than I had when I was Eric's age. They worked us hard in those days and kept us short of cash. Though even then – we broke out and had a bit of fun sometimes.

GERALD: I'll bet you did.

BIRLING *(solemnly):* But this is the point. I don't want to lecture you two young fellows again. But what so many of you don't seem to understand now, when things are so much easier, is that a man has to make his own way – has to look after himself – and his family too, of course, when he has one – and so long as he does that he won't come to much harm. But the way some of these cranks talk and write now, you'd think everybody has to look after everybody else, as if we were all mixed up together like bees in a hive – community and all that nonsense. But take my word for it, you youngsters – and I've learnt in the good hard school of experience – that a man has to mind his own business and look after himself and his own – and –

We hear the sharp ring of a front door bell. BIRLING *stops to listen.*

ERIC: Somebody at the front door.

BIRLING: Edna'll answer it. Well, have another glass of port, Gerald – and then we'll join the ladies. That'll stop me giving you good advice.

ERIC: Yes, you've piled it on a bit tonight, Father.

BIRLING: Special occasion. And feeling contented, for once, I wanted you to have the benefit of my experience.

EDNA *enters.*

* **token** *Zeichen*

fishy (coll), seeming false, doubtful

to get up to (coll) to be capable of, busy with

crank a person with strange, very unusual ideas

hive *Bienenkorb, -stock* /

* **benefit** advantage /

Bench member of a group of judges, here: police court (a law-court in which the less serious cases are heard)
***warrant** *Vollmacht*
to be up to to do sth bad
***awkward** causing difficulty
***defiant** *trotzig*
massiveness *Schwere*
solidity *Zuverlässigkeit*
purposefulness *Entschlossenheit*
weightily *gewichtig*
disconcerting confusing, embarrassing
***on duty** *im Dienst*
***to transfer** to move officially from one place, job to another
alderman *Ratsherr*

EDNA: Please, sir, an inspector's called.

BIRLING: An inspector? What kind of inspector?

EDNA: A police inspector. He says his name's Inspector Goole.

BIRLING: Don't know him. Does he want to see me?

EDNA: Yes, sir. He says it's important.

BIRLING: All right, Edna. Show him in here. Give us some more light.

EDNA *does, then goes out.*

I'm still on the Bench. It may be something about a warrant.

GERALD *(lightly)*: Sure to be. Unless Eric's been up to something. *(Nodding confidentially to* BIRLING.*)* And that would be awkward, wouldn't it?

BIRLING *(humorously)*: Very.

ERIC *(who is uneasy, sharply)*: Here, what do you mean?

GERALD *(lightly)*: Only something we were talking about when you were out. A joke really.

ERIC *(still uneasy)*: Well, I don't think it's very funny.

BIRLING *(sharply, staring at him)*: What's the matter with you?

ERIC *(defiantly)*: Nothing.

EDNA *(opening door, and announcing)*: Inspector Goole.

The INSPECTOR *enters, and* EDNA *goes, closing door after her. The* INSPECTOR *need not be a big man but he creates at once an impression of massiveness, solidity and purposefulness. He is a man in his fifties, dressed in a plain darkish suit of the period. He speaks carefully, weightily, and has a disconcerting habit of looking hard at the person he addresses before actually speaking.*

INSPECTOR: Mr Birling?

BIRLING: Yes. Sit down, Inspector.

INSPECTOR *(sitting)*: Thank you, sir.

BIRLING: Have a glass of port – or a little whisky?

INSPECTOR: No, thank you, Mr Birling. I'm on duty.

BIRLING: You're new, aren't you?

INSPECTOR: Yes, sir. Only recently transferred.

BIRLING: I thought you must be. I was an alderman for years – and Lord Mayor two years ago – and I'm still on the Bench – so I know the Brumley police officers pretty well – and I thought I'd never seen you before.

INSPECTOR: Quite so.

BIRLING: Well, what can I do for you? Some trouble about a warrant?

INSPECTOR: No, Mr Birling.

BIRLING *(after a pause, with a touch of impatience)*: Well, what is it then?

INSPECTOR: I'd like some information, if you don't mind, Mr Birling. Two hours ago a young woman died in the Infirmary. She'd been taken there this afternoon because she'd swallowed a lot of strong disinfectant. Burnt her inside out, of course.

ERIC *(involuntarily)*: My God!

INSPECTOR: Yes, she was in great agony. They did everything they could for her at the Infirmary, but she died. Suicide of course.

BIRLING *(rather impatiently)*: Yes yes. Horrible business. But I don't understand why you should come here, Inspector –

INSPECTOR *(cutting through, massively)*: I've been round to the room she had, and she'd left a letter there and a sort of diary. Like a lot of these young women who get into various kinds of trouble, she'd used more than one name. But her original name – her real name – was Eva Smith.

BIRLING *(thoughtfully)*: Eva Smith?

INSPECTOR: Do you remember her, Mr Birling?

BIRLING *(slowly)*: No – I seem to remember hearing that name – Eva Smith – somewhere. But it doesn't convey anything to me. And I don't see where I come into this.

INSPECTOR: She was employed in your works at one time.

BIRLING: Oh – that's it, is it? Well, we've several hundred young women there, y'know, and they keep changing.

INSPECTOR: This young woman, Eva Smith, was a bit out of the ordinary. I found a photograph of her in her lodgings. Perhaps you'd remember her from that.

INSPECTOR *takes a photograph, about postcard size, out of his pocket and goes to* BIRLING. *Both*

infirmary hospital

disinfectant a chemical used to destroy bacteria

*__involuntary__ without intention /

*__agony__ great pain or suffering /

*__suicide__ the act of killing oneself /

convey here: mean

lodgings (pl) the room(s) one pays rent for in a private house

to interpose to put between

***annoyed** angry
to annoy to cause trouble, make angry
annoyance

GERALD and ERIC rise to have a look at the photograph, but the INSPECTOR interposes himself between them and the photograph. They are surprised and rather annoyed. BIRLING stares hard, and with recognition, at the photograph, which the INSPECTOR then replaces in his pocket.

GERALD *(showing annoyance)*: Any particular reason why I shouldn't see this girl's photograph, Inspector?

INSPECTOR *(coolly, looking hard at him)*: There might be.

ERIC: And the same applies to me, I suppose?

INSPECTOR: Yes.

GERALD: I can't imagine what it could be.

ERIC: Neither can I.

BIRLING: And I must say, I agree with them, Inspector.

INSPECTOR: It's the way I like to go to work. One person and one line of enquiry at a time. Otherwise, there's a muddle.

***enquiry** also: inquiry the act of asking, finding out
muddle state of disorder

BIRLING: I see. Sensible really. *(Moves restlessly, then turns.)* You've had enough of that port, Eric.

The INSPECTOR is watching BIRLING and now BIRLING notices him.

***to employ** *beschäftigen*
employee *Arbeitnehmer*
employer *Arbeitgeber*
employment *Beschäftigung*

INSPECTOR: I think you remember Eva Smith now, don't you, Mr Birling?

BIRLING: Yes, I do. She was one of my employees and then I discharged her.

***to discharge** to dismiss, tell to go

ERIC: Is that why she committed suicide? When was this, Father?

BIRLING: Just keep quiet, Eric, and don't get excited. This girl left us nearly two years ago. Let me see – it must have been in the early autumn of nineteen-ten.

INSPECTOR: Yes. End of September, nineteen-ten.

BIRLING: That's right.

GERALD: Look here, sir. Wouldn't you rather I was out of this?

BIRLING: I don't mind your being here, Gerald. And I'm sure you've no objection, have you, Inspector? Perhaps I ought to explain first that this is Mr Gerald Croft – the son of Sir George Croft – you know, Crofts Limited.

INSPECTOR: Mr Gerald Croft, eh?

BIRLING: Yes. Incidentally we've been modestly celebrating his engagement to my daughter, Sheila.

INSPECTOR: I see. Mr Croft is going to marry Miss Sheila Birling?

GERALD *(smiling)*: I hope so.

INSPECTOR *(gravely)*: Then I'd prefer you to stay.

GERALD *(surprised)*: Oh – all right.

BIRLING *(somewhat impatiently)*: Look – there's nothing mysterious – or scandalous – about this business – at least not so far as I'm concerned. It's a perfectly straightforward case, and as it happened more than eighteen months ago – nearly two years ago – obviously it has nothing whatever to do with the wretched girl's suicide. Eh, Inspector?

INSPECTOR: No, sir. I can't agree with you there.

BIRLING: Why not?

INSPECTOR: Because what happened to her then may have determined what happened to her afterwards, and what happened to her afterwards may have driven her to suicide. A chain of events.

BIRLING: Oh well – put like that, there's something in what you say. Still, I can't accept any responsibility. If we were all responsible for everything that happened to everybody we'd had anything to do with, it would be very awkward, wouldn't it?

INSPECTOR: Very awkward.

BIRLING: We'd all be in an impossible position, wouldn't we?

ERIC: By Jove, yes. And as you were saying, Dad, a man has to look after himself –

BIRLING: Yes, well, we needn't go into all that.

INSPECTOR: Go into what?

BIRLING: Oh – just before you came – I'd been giving these young men a little good advice. Now – about this girl, Eva Smith. I remember her quite well now. She was a lively good-looking girl – country-bred, I fancy – and she'd been working in one of our machine shops for over a year. A good worker too. In fact, the foreman there told me he was ready to promote her into what we call a leading operator – head of a small group of girls. But after they came back from their holidays that August, they were all rather restless, and they suddenly decided to ask for more money. They were averaging about twenty-

incidentally *nebenbei bemerkt*
***modest** *bescheiden*

***straightforward** honest, without hidden meanings

wretched very unhappy, miserable

***to determine** to cause to find out, to fix
determination firm intention
determined showing strong will

awkward causing difficulty or uncomfortable feelings

By Jove! *Bei Gott!*

to go into to describe in detail

country-bred raised and educated in the country
to fancy to think
machine shop *Maschinenhalle*
foreman *Werkmeister*
leading operator *Vorarbeiterin*

to average here: *durchschnittlich verdienen*

rates (pl) standard of wages *(Tarif)*

shilling: money in use in Britain until 1971, equal to 12 (old) pence (= 5 new pence) and 1/20 of 1 pound

labour costs (pl) *Lohnkosten*

broke (sl) completely without money

ringleader *Rädelsführer*

to clear out to leave

tough luck (infml) too bad, unfortunate

two and six, which was neither more nor less than is paid generally in our industry. They wanted the rates raised so that they could average about twenty-five shillings a week. I refused, of course.

INSPECTOR: Why?

BIRLING *(surprised)*: Did you say "Why?"?

INSPECTOR: Yes. Why did you refuse?

BIRLING: Well, Inspector, I don't see that it's any concern of yours how I choose to run my business. Is it now?

INSPECTOR: It might be, you know.

BIRLING: I don't like the tone.

INSPECTOR: I'm sorry. But you asked me a question.

BIRLING: And you asked me a question before that, a quite unnecessary question too.

INSPECTOR: It's my duty to ask questions.

BIRLING: Well, it's my duty to keep labour costs down, and if I'd agreed to this demand for a new rate we'd have added about twelve per cent to our labour costs. Does that satisfy you? So I refused. Said I couldn't consider it. We were paying the usual rates and if they didn't like those rates, they could go and work somewhere else. It's a free country, I told them.

ERIC: It isn't if you can't go and work somewhere else.

INSPECTOR: Quite so.

BIRLING *(to* ERIC*)*: Look – just you keep out of this. You hadn't even started in the works when this happened. So they went on strike. That didn't last long, of course.

GERALD: Not if it was just after the holidays. They'd be all broke – if I know them.

BIRLING: Right, Gerald. They mostly were. And so was the strike, after a week or two. Pitiful affair. Well, we let them all come back – at the old rates – except the four or five ringleaders, who'd started the trouble. I went down myself and told them to clear out. And this girl, Eva Smith, was one of them. She'd had a lot to say – far too much – so she had to go.

GERALD: You couldn't have done anything else.

ERIC: He could. He could have kept her on instead of throwing her out. I call it tough luck.

Birling: Rubbish! If you don't come down sharply on some of these people, they'd soon be asking for the earth.

Gerald: I should say so!

Inspector: They might. But after all it's better to ask for the earth than to take it.

Birling *(staring at the* Inspector*)*: What did you say your name was, Inspector?

Inspector: Goole. G – double O – L – E.

Birling: How do you get on with our Chief Constable, Colonel Roberts?

Inspector: I don't see much of him.

Birling: Perhaps I ought to warn you that he's an old friend of mine, and that I see him fairly frequently. We play golf together sometimes up at the West Brumley.

Inspector *(dryly)*: I don't play golf.

Birling: I didn't suppose you did.

Eric *(bursting out)*: Well, I think it's a dam' shame.

Inspector: No, I've never wanted to play.

Eric: No. I mean about this girl – Eva Smith. Why shouldn't they try for higher wages? We try for the highest possible prices. And I don't see why she should have been sacked just because she'd a bit more spirit than the others. You said yourself she was a good worker. I'd have let her stay.

Birling *(rather angrily)*: Unless you brighten your ideas, you'll never be in a position to let anybody stay or to tell anybody to go. It's about time you learnt to face a few responsibilities. That's something this public-school-and-Varsity life you've had doesn't seem to teach you.

Eric *(sulkily)*: Well, we don't need to tell the Inspector all about that, do we?

Birling: I don't see we need to tell the Inspector anything more. In fact, there's nothing I can tell him. I told the girl to clear out, and she went. That's the last I heard of her. Have you any idea what happened to her after that? Get into trouble? Go on the streets?

Inspector *(rather slowly)*: No, she didn't exactly go on the streets.

Sheila *has now entered.*

Sheila *(gaily)*: What's this about streets? *(Noticing the* Inspector.*)* Oh – sorry. I didn't know. Mummy sent

***rubbish** nonsense

to come down on to ask forcefully, to criticize

Chief Constable officer in charge of the local police *(Polizeipräsident)*

Colonel *Oberst*

What is Mr Birling trying to do?

dam' (sl) damned

to sack (sl) to dismiss

***to brighten** to (cause to) become bright; here: change for the better

Varsity (coll) university

sulky *mürrisch, trotzend*

me in to ask you why you didn't come along to the drawing-room.

BIRLING: We shall be along in a minute now. Just finishing.

INSPECTOR: I'm afraid not.

BIRLING *(abruptly)*: There's nothing else, y'know. I've just told you that.

SHEILA: What's all this about?

BIRLING: Nothing to do with you, Sheila. Run along.

INSPECTOR: No, wait a minute, Miss Birling.

BIRLING *(angrily)*: Look here, Inspector, I consider this uncalled-for and officious. I've half a mind to report you. I've told you all I know – and it doesn't seem to me very important – and now there isn't the slightest reason why my daughter should be dragged into this unpleasant business.

SHEILA *(coming further in)*: What business? What's happening?

INSPECTOR *(impressively)*: I'm a police inspector, Miss Birling. This afternoon a young woman drank some disinfectant, and died, after several hours of agony, tonight in the Infirmary.

SHEILA: Oh – how horrible! Was it an accident?

INSPECTOR: No. She wanted to end her life. She felt she couldn't go on any longer.

BIRLING: Well, don't tell me that's because I discharged her from my employment nearly two years ago.

ERIC: That might have started it.

SHEILA: Did you, Dad?

BIRLING: Yes. The girl had been causing trouble in the works. I was quite justified.

GERALD: Yes, I think you were. I know we'd have done the same thing. Don't look like that, Sheila.

SHEILA *(rather distressed)*: Sorry! It's just that I can't help thinking about this girl – destroying herself so horribly – and I've been so happy tonight. Oh I wish you hadn't told me. What was she like? Quite young?

INSPECTOR: Yes. Twenty-four.

SHEILA: Pretty?

INSPECTOR: She wasn't pretty when I saw her today, but she had been pretty – very pretty.

BIRLING: That's enough of that.

---

drawing-room (fml) similar to living-room, a room in which people relax and guests are received and entertained

***abruptly** suddenly, impolitely

uncalled-for not right

officious too eager to give orders *(übertrieben diensteifrig)*

to have half a mind to have a desire or intention that is not firmly formed

***to report** to make a complaint about

***distressed** greatly worried, suffering

GERALD: And I don't really see that this enquiry gets you anywhere, Inspector. It's what happened to her since she left Mr Birling's works that is important.

BIRLING: Obviously. I suggested that some time ago.

GERALD: And we can't help you there because we don't know.

INSPECTOR *(slowly)*: Are you sure you don't know?

He looks at GERALD, *then at* ERIC, *then at* SHEILA.

BIRLING: And are you suggesting now that one of them knows something about this girl?

INSPECTOR: Yes.

BIRLING: You didn't come here just to see me then?

INSPECTOR: No.

The other four exchange bewildered and perturbed glances.

BIRLING *(with marked change of tone)*: Well, of course, if I'd known that earlier, I wouldn't have called you officious and talked about reporting you. You understand that, don't you, Inspector? I thought that – for some reason best known to yourself – you were making the most of this tiny bit of information I could give you. I'm sorry. This makes a difference. You sure of your facts?

INSPECTOR: Some of them – yes.

BIRLING: I can't think they can be of any great consequence.

INSPECTOR: The girl's dead though.

SHEILA: What do you mean by saying that? You talk as if we were responsible –

BIRLING *(cutting in)*: Just a minute, Sheila. Now, Inspector, perhaps you and I had better go and talk this over quietly in a corner –

SHEILA *(cutting in)*: Why should you? He's finished with you. He says it's one of us now.

BIRLING: Yes, and I'm trying to settle it sensibly for you.

GERALD: Well, there's nothing to settle as far as I'm concerned. I've never known an Eva Smith.

ERIC: Neither have I.

SHEILA: Was that her name? Eva Smith?

GERALD: Yes.

SHEILA: Never heard it before.

*__bewildered__ confused
perturbed greatly disturbed
glance a rapid look

*__to make the most of__ to gain as much advantage as one can
you sure (coll) Are you sure?

though here: however

to settle to fix, make arrangements
*__sensible__ *vernünftig*

***to despair** to lose all hope
despair complete lack or loss of hope
desperate *verzweifelt*
desperation the state of being desperate

rotten (sl) very bad

warehouse large building for storing things to be sold

notion idea

dingy dirty and dark

stroke of luck *Glückstreffer*

archly making fun of people in a playful way

GERALD: So where are you now, Inspector?

INSPECTOR: Where I was before, Mr Croft. I told you – that like a lot of these young women, she'd used more than one name. She was still Eva Smith when Mr Birling sacked her – for wanting twenty-five shillings a week instead of twenty-two and six. But after that she stopped being Eva Smith. Perhaps she'd had enough of it.

ERIC: Can't blame her.

SHEILA *(to* BIRLING*)*: I think it was a mean thing to do. Perhaps that spoilt everything for her.

BIRLING: Rubbish! *(To* INSPECTOR.*)* Do you know what happened to this girl after she left my works?

INSPECTOR: Yes. She was out of work for the next two months. Both her parents were dead, so that she'd no home to go back to. And she hadn't been able to save much out of what Birling and Company had paid her. So that after two months, with no work, no money coming in, and living in lodgings, with no relatives to help her, few friends, lonely, half-starved, she was feeling desperate.

SHEILA *(warmly)*: I should think so. It's a rotten shame.

INSPECTOR: There are a lot of young women living that sort of existence in every city and big town in this country, Miss Birling. If there weren't, the factories and warehouses wouldn't know where to look for cheap labour. Ask your father.

SHEILA: But these girls aren't cheap labour – they're *people*.

INSPECTOR *(dryly)*: I've had that notion myself from time to time. In fact, I've thought that it would do us all a bit of good if sometimes we tried to put ourselves in the place of these young women counting their pennies in their dingy little back bedrooms.

SHEILA: Yes, I expect it would. But what happened to her then?

INSPECTOR: She had what seemed to her a wonderful stroke of luck. She was taken on in a shop – and a good shop too – Milwards.

SHEILA: Milwards! We go there – in fact, I was there this afternoon – *(archly to* GERALD*)* for *your* benefit.

GERALD *(smiling)*: Good!

SHEILA: Yes, she was lucky to get taken on at Milwards.

INSPECTOR: That's what she thought. And it happened that at the beginning of December that year – nineteen-ten – there was a good deal of influenza about, and Milwards suddenly found themselves short-handed. So that gave her her chance. It seems she liked working there. It was a nice change from a factory. She enjoyed being among pretty clothes, I've no doubt. And now she felt she was making a good fresh start. You can imagine how she felt.

SHEILA: Yes, of course.

BIRLING: And then she got herself into trouble there, I suppose?

INSPECTOR: After about a couple of months, just when she felt she was settling down nicely, they told her she'd have to go.

BIRLING: Not doing her work properly?

INSPECTOR: There was nothing wrong with the way she was doing her work. They admitted that.

BIRLING: There must have been something wrong.

INSPECTOR: All she knew was – that a customer complained about her – and so she had to go.

SHEILA *(staring at him, agitated)*: When was this?

INSPECTOR *(impressively)*: At the end of January – last year.

SHEILA: What – what did this girl look like?

INSPECTOR: If you'll come over here, I'll show you.

He moves nearer a light – perhaps standard lamp – and she crosses to him. He produces the photograph. She looks at it closely, recognises it with a little cry, gives a half-stifled sob, and then runs out. The INSPECTOR *puts the photograph back into his pocket and stares speculatively after her. The other three stare in amazement for a moment.*

BIRLING: What's the matter with her?

ERIC: She recognised her from the photograph, didn't she?

INSPECTOR: Yes.

BIRLING *(angrily)*: Why the devil do you want to go upsetting the child like that?

INSPECTOR: I didn't do it. She's upsetting herself.

BIRLING: Well – why – why?

INSPECTOR: I don't know – yet. That's something I have to find out.

short-handed lacking the required number of workers or employees

standard lamp *Stehlampe*

half-stifled partly suppressed

***speculative** *nachdenklich, grüblerisch*

***amazement** great surprise

***to upset** to confuse, worry

BIRLING *(still angrily)*: Well – if you don't mind – I'll find out first.

GERALD: Shall I go to her?

BIRLING *(moving)*: No, leave this to me. I must also have a word with my wife – tell her what's happening. *(Turns at door, staring at* INSPECTOR *angrily.)* We were having a nice little family celebration tonight. And a nasty mess you've made of it now, haven't you?

/ ***mess** state of disorder

INSPECTOR *(steadily)*: That's more or less what I was thinking earlier tonight, when I was in the Infirmary looking at what was left of Eva Smith. A nice little promising life there, I thought, and a nasty mess somebody's made of it.

BIRLING looks as if about to make some retort, then thinks better of it, and goes out, closing door sharply behind him. GERALD and ERIC exchange uneasy glances. The INSPECTOR ignores them.

retort a quick, rather angry answer
to think better of to change one's mind

GERALD: I'd like to have a look at that photograph now, Inspector.

INSPECTOR: All in good time.

all in good time *alles zu seiner Zeit*

GERALD: I don't see why –

INSPECTOR *(cutting in, massively)*: You heard what I said before, Mr Croft. One line of enquiry at a time. Otherwise we'll all be talking at once and won't know where we are. If you've anything to tell me, you'll have an opportunity of doing it soon.

GERALD *(rather uneasily)*: Well, I don't suppose I have –

ERIC *(suddenly bursting out)*: Look here, I've had enough of this.

INSPECTOR *(dryly)*: I dare say.

ERIC *(uneasily)*: I'm sorry – but you see – we were having a little party – and I've had a few drinks, including rather a lot of champagne – and I've got a headache – and as I'm only in the way here – I think I'd better turn in.

to turn in (coll) to go to bed

INSPECTOR: And I think you'd better stay here.

ERIC: Why should I?

INSPECTOR: It might be less trouble. If you turn in, you might have to turn out again soon.

GERALD: Getting a bit heavy-handed, aren't you, Inspector?

heavy-handed rather unkind and unfair in one's treatment of others

INSPECTOR: Possibly. But if you're easy with me, I'm easy with you.

GERALD: After all, y'know, we're respectable citizens and not criminals.

INSPECTOR: Sometimes there isn't as much difference as you think. Often, if it was left to me, I wouldn't know where to draw the line.

GERALD: Fortunately, it isn't left to you, is it?

INSPECTOR: No, it isn't. But some things are left to me. Enquiries of this sort, for instance. *(Enter* SHEILA, *who looks as if she's been crying.)* Well, Miss Birling?

SHEILA *(coming in, closing door)*: You knew it was me all the time, didn't you?

INSPECTOR: I had an idea it might be – from something the girl herself wrote.

SHEILA: I've told my father – he didn't seem to think it amounted to much – but I felt rotten about it at the time and now I feel a lot worse. Did it make much difference to her?

INSPECTOR: Yes, I'm afraid it did. It was the last real steady job she had. When she lost it – for no reason that she could discover – she decided she might as well try another kind of life.

SHEILA *(miserably)*: So I'm really responsible?

INSPECTOR: No, not entirely. A good deal happened to her after that. But you're partly to blame. Just as your father is.

ERIC: But what did Sheila do?

SHEILA *(distressed)*: I went to the manager at Milwards and I told him that if they didn't get rid of that girl, I'd never go near the place again and I'd persuade mother to close our account with them.

INSPECTOR: And why did you do that?

SHEILA: Because I was in a furious temper.

INSPECTOR: And what had this girl done to make you lose your temper?

SHEILA: When I was looking at myself in the mirror I caught sight of her smiling at the assistant, and I was furious with her. I'd been in a bad temper anyhow.

INSPECTOR: And was it the girl's fault?

SHEILA: No, not really. It was my own fault. (*Suddenly, to* GERALD*)* All right, Gerald, you needn't look at

to amount to much to be important
rotten (coll) bad

***account** *Konto*

***temper** state of mind, mood

***to lose one's temper** to become furious

me like that. At least, I'm trying to tell the truth. I expect you've done things you're ashamed of too.

GERALD *(surprised)*: Well, I never said I hadn't. I don't see why –

INSPECTOR *(cutting in)*: Never mind about that. You can settle that between you afterwards. *(To* SHEILA.*)* What happened?

SHEILA: I'd gone in to try something on. It was an idea of my own – mother had been against it, and so had the assistant – but I insisted. As soon as I tried it on, I knew they'd been right. It just didn't suit me at all. I looked silly in the thing. Well, this girl had brought the dress up from the workroom, and when the assistant – Miss Francis – had asked her something about it, this girl, to show us what she meant, had held the dress up, as if she was wearing it. And it just suited her. She was the right type for it, just as I was the wrong type. She was a very pretty girl too – with big dark eyes – and that didn't make it any better. Well, when I tried the thing on and looked at myself and knew that it was all wrong, I caught sight of this girl smiling at Miss Francis – as if to say: "Doesn't she look awful" – and I was absolutely furious. I was very rude to both of them, and then I went to the manager and told him that this girl had been very impertinent – and – and – *(She almost breaks down, but just controls herself.)* How could I know what would happen afterwards? If she'd been some miserable plain little creature, I don't suppose I'd have done it. But she was very pretty and looked as if she could take care of herself. I couldn't be sorry for her.

INSPECTOR: In fact, in a kind of way, you might be said to have been jealous of her.

SHEILA: Yes, I suppose so.

INSPECTOR: And so you used the power you had, as a daughter of a good customer and also of a man well-known in the town, to punish the girl just because she made you feel like that?

SHEILA: Yes, but it didn't seem to be anything very terrible at the time. Don't you understand? And if I could help her now, I would –

INSPECTOR *(harshly)*: Yes, but you can't. It's too late. She's dead.

***(shop) assistant** person who serves customers

/ ***impertinent** rude or disrespectful, impolite

***plain** not pretty

ERIC: My God, it's a bit thick, when you come to think of it –

SHEILA *(stormily)*: Oh shut up, Eric. I know, I know. It's the only time I've ever done anything like that, and I'll never, never do it again to anybody. I've noticed them giving me a sort of look sometimes at Milwards – I noticed it even this afternoon – and I suppose some of them remember. I feel now I can never go there again. Oh – why had this to happen?

INSPECTOR *(sternly)*: That's what I asked myself to-night when I was looking at that dead girl. And then I said to myself: "Well, we'll try to understand why it had to happen." And that's why I'm here, and why I'm not going until I know *all* that happened. Eva Smith lost her job with Birling and Company because the strike failed and they were determined not to have another one. At last she found another job – under what name I don't know – in a big shop, and had to leave there because you were annoyed with yourself and passed the annoyance on to her. Now she had to try something else. So first she changed her name to Daisy Renton –

GERALD *(startled)*: What?

INSPECTOR *(steadily)*: I said she changed her name to Daisy Renton.

GERALD *(pulling himself together)*: D'you mind if I give myself a drink, Sheila?

SHEILA *merely nods, still staring at him, and he goes across to the tantalus on the sideboard for a whisky.*

INSPECTOR: Where is your father, Miss Birling?

SHEILA: He went into the drawing-room, to tell my mother what was happening here. Eric, take the Inspector along to the drawing-room. *(As* ERIC *moves, the* INSPECTOR *looks from* SHEILA *to* GERALD, *then goes out with* ERIC.*)* Well, Gerald?

GERALD *(trying to smile)*: Well what, Sheila?

SHEILA: How did you come to know this girl – Eva Smith?

GERALD: I didn't.

SHEILA: Daisy Renton then – it's the same thing.

GERALD: Why should I have known her?

a bit thick (sl) beyond what is reasonable, unfair

stormy showing noisy expressions of feeling

stern showing firmness, esp. with disapproval

* **to be determined** to have or show a strong will /

to startle *erschrecken*
< What does Gerald's reaction show?

tantalus *Vitrine*

to give oneself away to tell (a secret) unintentionally, to make known the truth about sth

SHEILA: Oh don't be stupid. We haven't much time. You gave yourself away as soon as he mentioned her other name.

GERALD: All right. I knew her. Let's leave it at that.

SHEILA: We can't leave it at that.

GERALD *(approaching her)*: Now listen, darling –

SHEILA: No, that's no use. You not only knew her but you knew her very well. Otherwise, you wouldn't look so guilty about it. When did you first get to know her? *(He does not reply.)* Was it after she left Milwards? When she changed her name, as he said, and began to lead a different sort of life? Were you seeing her last spring and summer, during that time when you hardly came near me and said you were so busy? Were you? *(He does not reply but looks at her.)* Yes, of course you were.

over and done with completely finished

GERALD: I'm sorry, Sheila. But it was all over and done with, last summer, I hadn't set eyes on the girl for at least six months. I don't come into this suicide business.

SHEILA: I thought I didn't, half an hour ago.

GERALD: You don't. Neither of us does. So – for God's sake – don't say anything to the Inspector.

SHEILA: About you and this girl?

GERALD: Yes. We can keep it from him.

SHEILA *(laughs rather hysterically)*: Why – you fool – *he knows*. Of course he knows. And I hate to think how much he knows that we don't know yet. You'll see. You'll see.

crushed utterly defeated

She looks at him almost in triumph. He looks crushed. The door slowly opens and the INSPECTOR *appears, looking steadily and searchingly at them.*

INSPECTOR: Well?

How do you think the play will go on? Make some notes.

End of Act One

Act Two

At rise, scene and situation are exactly as they were at end of Act I.

The INSPECTOR *remains at the door for a few moments looking at* SHEILA *and* GERALD. *Then he comes forward, leaving door open behind him.*

INSPECTOR *(to* GERALD*)*: Well?

SHEILA *(with hysterical laugh, to* GERALD*)*: You see? What did I tell you?

INSPECTOR: What did you tell him?

GERALD *(with an effort)*: Inspector, I think Miss Birling ought to be excused any more of this questioning. She's nothing more to tell you. She's had a long, exciting and tiring day – we were celebrating our engagement, you know – and now she's obviously had about as much as she can stand. You heard her.

ought to be excused should be freed from

SHEILA: He means that I'm getting hysterical now.

INSPECTOR: And are you?

SHEILA: Probably.

INSPECTOR: Well, I don't want to keep you here. I've no more questions to ask you.

SHEILA: No, but you haven't finished asking questions – have you?

INSPECTOR: No.

SHEILA *(to* GERALD*)*: You see? *(To* INSPECTOR.*)* Then I'm staying.

GERALD: Why should you? It's bound to be unpleasant and disturbing.

* **bound to** certain, sure

INSPECTOR: And you think young women ought to be protected against unpleasant and disturbing things?

GERALD: If possible – yes.

➤ Why does Gerald want Sheila to leave?

INSPECTOR: Well, we know one young woman who wasn't, don't we?

GERALD: I suppose I asked for that.

SHEILA: Be careful you don't ask for any more, Gerald.

to ask for it (coll) to behave in a way that is likely to result in trouble for oneself

GERALD: I only meant to say to you – Why stay when you'll hate it?

SHEILA: It can't be any worse for me than it has been. And it might be better.

GERALD *(bitterly)*: I see.

SHEILA: What do you see?

GERALD: You've been through it – and now you want to see somebody else put through it.

SHEILA *(bitterly)*: So that's what you think I'm really like. I'm glad I realised it in time, Gerald.

GERALD: No, no, I didn't mean –

SHEILA *(cutting in)*: Yes, you did. And if you'd really loved me, you couldn't have said that. You listened to that nice story about me. I got that girl sacked from Milwards. And now you've made up your mind I must obviously be a selfish, vindictive creature.

vindictive *rachsüchtig*

GERALD: I neither said that nor even suggested it.

SHEILA: Then why say I want to see somebody else put through it? That's not what I meant at all.

GERALD: All right then, I'm sorry.

SHEILA: Yes, but you don't believe me. And this is just the wrong time not to believe me.

INSPECTOR *(massively taking charge)*: Allow me, Miss Birling. (*To* GERALD.) I can tell you why Miss Birling wants to stay on and why she says it might be better for her if she did. A girl died tonight. A pretty, lively sort of girl, who never did anybody no harm. But she died in misery and agony – hating life –

to take charge to take the matter in hand

no harm any harm

SHEILA *(distressed)*: Don't please – I know, I know – and I can't stop thinking about it –

INSPECTOR *(ignoring this)*: Now Miss Birling has just been made to understand what she did to this girl. She feels responsible. And if she leaves us now, and doesn't hear any more, then she'll feel she's entirely to blame, she'll be alone with her responsibility, the rest of tonight, all tomorrow, all the next night –

SHEILA *(eagerly)*: Yes, that's it. And I know I'm to blame – and I'm desperately sorry – but I can't believe – I won't believe – it's simply my fault that in the end she – she committed suicide. That would be too horrible –

INSPECTOR *(sternly to them both)*: You see, we have to share something. If there's nothing else, we'll have to share our guilt.

SHEILA *(staring at him)*: Yes. That's true. You know. *(She goes closer to him, wonderingly.)* I don't understand about you.

INSPECTOR *(calmly)*: There's no reason why you should.

He regards her calmly while she stares at him wonderingly and dubiously. Now MRS. BIRLING *enters, briskly and self-confidently, quite out of key with the little scene that has just passed.* SHEILA *feels this at once.*

MRS BIRLING *(smiling, social)*: Good evening, Inspector.

INSPECTOR: Good evening, madam.

MRS BIRLING *(same easy tone)*: I'm Mrs Birling, y'know. My husband has just explained why you're here, and while we'll be glad to tell you anything you want to know, I don't think we can help you much.

SHEILA: No, Mother – please!

MRS BIRLING *(affecting great surprise)*: What's the matter, Sheila?

SHEILA *(hesitantly)*: I know it sounds silly –

MRS BIRLING: What does?

SHEILA: You see, I feel you're beginning all wrong. And I'm afraid you'll say something or do something that you'll be sorry for afterwards.

MRS BIRLING: I don't know what you're talking about, Sheila.

SHEILA: We all started like that – so confident, so pleased with ourselves until he began asking us questions.

MRS BIRLING *looks from* SHEILA *to the* INSPECTOR.

MRS BIRLING: You seem to have made a great impression on this child, Inspector.

INSPECTOR *(coolly)*: We often do on the young ones. They're more impressionable.

He and MRS BIRLING *look at each other for a moment. Then* MRS BIRLING *turns to* SHEILA *again.*

MRS BIRLING: You're looking tired, dear. I think you ought to go to bed – and forget about this absurd business. You'll feel better in the morning.

***dubious** feeling uncertain

***brisk** lively

out of key *nicht in Einklang*

social *gesellig*

***to affect** to pretend to feel *(heucheln)*

***hesitant** hesitating *(zögernd)*

***impressionable** easy to influence

***absurd** foolish

to settle to decide on
morbid unhealthy, unnatural
/ ★**curiosity** *Neugier*
haughty arrogant
plain clear
a trifle rather
/ **impertinent** rude, disrespectful
to take offence to feel annoyed, to attack
to rebuke to blame
to conduct to lead

SHEILA: Mother, I couldn't possibly go. Nothing could be worse for me. We've settled all that. I'm staying here until I know why that girl killed herself.

MRS BIRLING: Nothing but morbid curiosity.

SHEILA: No it isn't.

MRS BIRLING: Please don't contradict me like that. And in any case I don't suppose for a moment that we can understand why the girl committed suicide. Girls of that class –

SHEILA *(urgently, cutting in)*: Mother, don't – please don't. For your own sake, as well as ours, you mustn't –

MRS BIRLING *(annoyed)*: Mustn't – what? Really, Sheila!

SHEILA *(slowly, carefully now)*: You mustn't try to build up a kind of wall between us and that girl. If you do, then the Inspector will just break it down. And it'll be all the worse when he does.

MRS BIRLING: I don't understand you. *(To* INSPECTOR.*)* Do you?

INSPECTOR: Yes. And she's right.

MRS BIRLING *(haughtily)*: I beg your pardon!

INSPECTOR *(very plainly)*: I said Yes – I do understand her. And she's right.

MRS BIRLING: That – I consider – is a trifle impertinent, Inspector. *(*SHEILA *gives short hysterical laugh.)* Now, what is it, Sheila?

SHEILA: I don't know. Perhaps it's because *impertinent* is such a silly word.

MRS BIRLING: In any case ...

SHEILA: But, Mother, do stop before it's too late.

MRS BIRLING: If you mean that the Inspector will take offence –

INSPECTOR *(cutting in, calmly)*: No, no. I never take offence.

MRS BIRLING: I'm glad to hear it. Though I must add that it seems to me that we have more reason for taking offence.

INSPECTOR: Let's leave *offence* out of it, shall we?

GERALD: I think we'd better.

SHEILA: So do I.

MRS BIRLING *(rebuking them)*: *I'm* talking to the Inspector now, if you don't mind. *(To* INSPECTOR, *rather grandly.)* I realise that you may have to conduct some sort of enquiry, but I must say that so far you seem to be conducting it in a rather peculiar and offensive manner. You know of course that my husband was Lord Mayor only two years ago and that he's still a magistrate –

GERALD *(cutting in, rather impatiently)*: Miss Birling, the Inspector knows all that. And I don't think it's a very good idea to remind him –

SHEILA *(cutting in)*: It's crazy. Stop it, please, Mother.

INSPECTOR *(imperturbable)*: Yes. Now what about Mr Birling?

MRS BIRLING: He's coming back in a moment. He's just talking to my son, Eric, who seems to be in an excitable silly mood.

INSPECTOR: What's the matter with him?

MRS BIRLING: Eric? Oh – I'm afraid he may have had rather too much to drink tonight. We were having a little celebration here –

INSPECTOR *(cutting in)*: Isn't he used to drinking?

MRS BIRLING: No, of course not. He's only a boy.

INSPECTOR: No, he's a young man. And some young men drink far too much.

SHEILA: And Eric's one of them.

MRS BIRLING *(very sharply)*: Sheila!

SHEILA *(urgently)*: I don't want to get poor Eric into trouble. He's probably in enough trouble already. But we really must stop these silly pretences. This isn't the time to pretend that Eric isn't used to drink. He's been steadily drinking too much for the last two years.

MRS BIRLING *(staggered)*: It isn't true. You know him, Gerald – and you're a man – you must know it isn't true.

INSPECTOR *(as* GERALD *hesitates)*: Well, Mr Croft?

GERALD *(apologetically, to* MRS BIRLING*)*: I'm afraid it is, y'know. Actually I've never seen much of him outside this house – but – well, I have gathered that he does drink pretty hard.

MRS BIRLING *(bitterly)*: And this is the time you choose to tell me.

SHEILA: Yes, of course it is. That's what I meant when I talked about building up a wall that's sure to be knocked flat. It makes it all the harder to bear.

offensive unpleasant

magistrate an official judge (of the lowest rank)

imperturbable *unbewegt*

* **pretence** false appearance

staggered deeply shocked

* **apologetically** showing regret
apologetic
to apologize to express sorrow
apology (to sb) (for sth)

flat down

MRS BIRLING: But it's you – and not the Inspector here – who's doing it –

SHEILA: Yes, but don't you see? *He hasn't started on you yet.*

MRS BIRLING *(after pause, recovering herself)*: If necessary I shall be glad to answer any questions the Inspector wishes to ask me. Though naturally I don't know anything about this girl.

INSPECTOR *(gravely)*: We'll see, Mrs Birling.

Enter BIRLING, *who closes door behind him.*

bothered worried

BIRLING *(rather hot, bothered)*: I've been trying to persuade Eric to go to bed, but he won't. Now he says you told him to stay up. Did you?

INSPECTOR: Yes, I did.

BIRLING: Why?

INSPECTOR: Because I shall want to talk to him, Mr Birling.

lad boy

BIRLING: I can't see why you should, but if you must, then I suggest you do it now. Have him in and get it over, then let the lad go.

INSPECTOR: No, I can't do that yet. I'm sorry, but he'll have to wait.

BIRLING: Now look here, Inspector –

INSPECTOR *(cutting in, with authority)*: He must wait his turn.

SHEILA *(to* MRS BIRLING*)*: You see?

MRS BIRLING: No, I don't. And please be quiet, Sheila.

*__to propose__ to intend
to give sb rope to allow sb freedom to act

BIRLING *(angrily)*: Inspector, I've told you before, I don't like your tone nor the way you're handling this enquiry. And I don't propose to give you much more rope.

INSPECTOR: You needn't give me any rope.

SHEILA *(rather wildly, with laugh)*: No, he's giving us rope – so that we'll hang ourselves.

BIRLING *(to* MRS BIRLING*)*: What's the matter with that child?

MRS BIRLING: Over-excited. And she refused to go. *(With sudden anger, to* INSPECTOR.*)* Well, come along – what is it you want to know?

/ **to compel** to make sb do sth

INSPECTOR *(coolly)*: At the end of January, last year, this girl Eva Smith had to leave Milwards, because Miss Birling compelled them to discharge her, and then she stopped being Eva Smith, looking for a job, and became Daisy Renton, with other ideas. *(Sharply turning on him.)* Mr Croft, when did you first get to know her?

An exclamation of surprise from BIRLING *and* MRS BIRLING.

GERALD: Where did you get the idea that I did know her?

SHEILA: It's no use, Gerald. You're wasting time.

INSPECTOR: As soon as I mentioned the name Daisy Renton, it was obvious you'd known her. You gave yourself away at once.

SHEILA *(bitterly)*: Of course he did.

INSPECTOR: And anyhow I knew already. When and where did you first meet her?

GERALD: All right, if you must have it. I met her first, sometime in March last year, in the stalls bar at the Palace. I mean the Palace music hall here in Brumley –

SHEILA: Well, we didn't think you meant Buckingham Palace.

GERALD *(to* SHEILA*)*: Thanks. You're going to be a great help, I can see. You've said your piece, and you're obviously going to hate this, so why on earth don't you leave us to it?

SHEILA: Nothing would induce me. I want to understand exactly what happens when a man says he's so busy at the works that he can hardly ever find time to come and see the girl he's supposed to be in love with. I wouldn't miss it for worlds –

INSPECTOR *(with authority)*: Yes, Mr Croft – in the stalls bar at the Palace Variety Theatre ...

GERALD: I happened to look in, one night, after a rather long dull day, and as the show wasn't very bright, I went down into the bar for a drink. It's a favourite haunt of women of the town –

MRS BIRLING: Women of the town?

BIRLING: Yes, yes. But I see no point in mentioning the subject – especially – *(indicating* SHEILA.*)*

MRS BIRLING: It would be much better if Sheila didn't listen to this story at all.

SHEILA: But you're forgetting I'm supposed to be engaged to the hero of it. Go on, Gerald. You went

stalls the seats in a theatre nearest to the stage
stalls bar bar for those people in the stalls *(Sperrsitz)*
music hall *Varieté(theater)*

to induce to cause

haunt *Lieblingsplatz, Treffpunkt*
woman of the town prostitute

down into the bar, which is a favourite haunt of women of the town.

GERALD: I'm glad I amuse you –

INSPECTOR *(sharply)*: Come along, Mr Croft. What happened?

GERALD: I didn't propose to stay long down there. I hate those hard-eyed dough-faced women. But then I noticed a girl who looked quite different. She was very pretty – soft brown hair and big dark eyes – *(breaks off)* My God!

INSPECTOR: What's the matter?

GERALD *(distressed)*: Sorry – I – well, I've suddenly realised – taken it in properly – that she's dead –

INSPECTOR *(harshly)*: Yes, she's dead.

SHEILA: And probably between us we killed her.

MRS BIRLING *(sharply)*: Sheila, don't talk nonsense.

SHEILA: You wait, Mother.

INSPECTOR *(to* GERALD*)*: Go on.

GERALD: She looked young and fresh and charming and altogether out of place down there. And obviously she wasn't enjoying herself. Old Joe Meggarty, half-drunk and goggle-eyed, had wedged her into a corner with that obscene fat carcass of his –

MRS BIRLING *(cutting in)*: There's no need to be disgusting. And surely you don't mean Alderman Meggarty?

GERALD: Of course I do. He's a notorious womaniser as well as being one of the worst sots and rogues in Brumley –

INSPECTOR: Quite right.

MRS BIRLING *(staggered)*: Well, really! Alderman Meggarty! I must say, we are learning something tonight.

SHEILA *(coolly)*: Of course we are. But everybody knows about that horrible old Meggarty. A girl I know had to see him at the Town Hall one afternoon and she only escaped with a torn blouse –

BIRLING *(sharply, shocked)*: Sheila!

INSPECTOR *(to* GERALD*)*: Go on, please.

GERALD: The girl saw me looking at her and then gave me a glance that was nothing less than a cry for help. So I went across and told Joe Meggarty some nonsense – that the manager had a message for him or something like that – got him out of the way –

dough-faced a face bearing little expression

to take in here: to understand

goggle-eyed *glotzäugig*
to wedge to fix firmly
obscene dirty, filthy
carcass *Kadaver*
alderman *Ratsherr*

notorious widely known
womaniser *Schürzenjäger*
sot person who is habitually drunk
rogue dishonest man

and then told the girl that if she didn't want any more of that sort of thing, she'd better let me take her out of there. She agreed at once.

INSPECTOR: Where did you go?

GERALD: We went along the County Hotel, which I knew would be quiet at that time of night, and we had a drink or two and talked.

INSPECTOR: Did she drink much at that time?

GERALD: No. She only had a port and lemonade – or some such concoction. All she wanted was to talk – a little friendliness – and I gathered that Joe Meggarty's advances had left her rather shaken – as well they might –

INSPECTOR: She talked about herself?

GERALD: Yes. I asked her questions about herself. She told me her name was Daisy Renton, that she'd lost both parents, that she came originally from somewhere outside Brumley. She also told me she'd had a job in one of the works here and had had to leave after a strike. She said something about the shop too, but wouldn't say which it was, and she was deliberately vague about what happened. I couldn't get any exact details from her about her past life. She wanted to talk about herself – just because she felt I was interested and friendly – but at the same time she wanted to be Daisy Renton – and not Eva Smith. In fact, I heard that name for the first time tonight. What she did let slip – though she didn't mean to – was that she was desperately hard up and at that moment was actually hungry. I made the people at the County find some food for her.

INSPECTOR: And then you decided to keep her – as your mistress?

MRS BIRLING: What?

SHEILA: Of course, Mother. It was obvious from the start. Go on, Gerald. Don't mind Mother.

GERALD *(steadily)*: I discovered, not that night but two nights later, when we met again – not accidentally this time of course – that in fact she hadn't a penny and was going to be turned out of the miserable back room she had. It happened that a friend of mine, Charlie Brunswick, had gone off to Canada for six months and had let me have the key of a nice little set of rooms he had – in Morgan Terrace – and

concoction mixed drink

advances (pl) approaches *(Annäherungsversuche)*

***deliberate** intentional, on purpose
to be vague not clearly described, expressed

hard up short of money

mistress *Geliebte*

***accidentally** by chance

had asked me to keep an eye on them for him and use them if I wanted to. So I insisted on Daisy moving into those rooms and I made her take some money to keep her going there. *(Carefully, to the* INSPECTOR*)* I want you to understand that I didn't install her there so that I could make love to her. I made her go to Morgan Terrace because I was sorry for her, and didn't like the idea of her going back to the Palace bar. I didn't ask for anything in return.

INSPECTOR: I see.

SHEILA: Yes, but why are you saying that to him? You ought to be saying it to me.

GERALD: I suppose I ought really. I'm sorry, Sheila. Somehow I –

SHEILA *(cutting in, as he hesitates)*: I know. Somehow he makes you.

INSPECTOR: But she became your mistress?

GERALD: Yes, I suppose it was inevitable. She was young and pretty and warm-hearted – and intensely grateful. I became at once the most important person in her life – you understand?

INSPECTOR: Yes. She was a woman. She was lonely. Were you in love with her?

SHEILA: Just what I was going to ask!

BIRLING *(angrily)*: I really must protest –

INSPECTOR *(turning on him sharply)*: Why should you do any protesting? It was you who turned the girl out in the first place.

BIRLING *(rather taken aback)*: Well, I only did what any employer might have done. And what I was going to say was that I protest against the way in which my daughter, a young unmarried girl, is being dragged into this –

INSPECTOR *(sharply)*: Your daughter isn't living on the moon. She's here in Brumley too.

SHEILA: Yes, and it was I who had the girl turned out of her job at Milwards. *And* I'm supposed to be engaged to Gerald. And I'm not a child, don't forget. I've a right to know. *Were* you in love with her, Gerald?

GERALD *(hesitatingly)*: It's hard to say. I didn't feel about her as she felt about me.

SHEILA *(with sharp sarcasm)*: Of course not. You were the wonderful Fairy Prince. You must have adored it, Gerald.

to keep her going to keep her alive

to take sb aback (esp. passive) to shock or surprise sb

to drag into here: *verwickeln*

Fairy Prince prince in a fairy-tale

***to adore** to love deeply; here: to enjoy very much

GERALD: All right – I did for a time. Nearly any man would have done.

SHEILA: That's probably about the best thing you've said tonight. At least it's honest. Did you go and see her every night?

GERALD: No. I wasn't telling you a complete lie when I said I'd been very busy at the works all that time. We were very busy. But of course I did see a good deal of her.

MRS BIRLING: I don't think we want any further details of this disgusting affair –

SHEILA *(cutting in)*: I do. And, anyhow, we haven't had any details yet.

GERALD: And you're not going to have any. *(To* MRS BIRLING.*)* You know, it wasn't disgusting.

MRS BIRLING: It's disgusting to me.

SHEILA: Yes, but after all, you didn't come into this, did you, Mother?

GERALD: Is there anything else you want to know – that you ought to know?

INSPECTOR: Yes, When did this affair end?

GERALD: I can tell you exactly. In the first week of September. I had to go away for several weeks then – on business – and by that time Daisy knew it was coming to an end. So I broke it off definitely before I went.

INSPECTOR: How did she take it?

GERALD: Better than I'd hoped. She was – very gallant – about it.

SHEILA *(with irony)*: That was nice for you.

GERALD: No, it wasn't. *(He waits a moment, then in low, troubled tone.)* She told me she'd been happier than she'd ever been before – but that she knew it couldn't last – hadn't expected it to last. She didn't blame me at all. I wish to God she had now. Perhaps I'd feel better about it.

INSPECTOR: She had to move out of those rooms?

GERALD: Yes, we'd agreed about that. She'd saved a little money during the summer – she'd lived very economically on what I'd allowed her – and didn't want to take any more from me, but I insisted on a parting gift of enough money – though it wasn't so very much – to see her through to the end of the year.

*__disgusting__ very unpleasant, terrible

gallant brave, showing courage

to allow to give, esp money

to see through to support or help until the end of (a time or difficulty) *to propose to suggest

INSPECTOR: Did she tell you what she proposed to do after you'd left her?

GERALD: No. She refused to talk about that. I got the idea, once or twice from what she said, that she thought of leaving Brumley. Whether she did or not – I don't know. Did she?

INSPECTOR: Yes. She went away for about two months. To some seaside place.

GERALD: By herself?

INSPECTOR: Yes. I think she went away – to be alone, to be quiet, to remember all that had happened between you.

GERALD: How do you know that?

INSPECTOR: She kept a rough sort of diary. And she said there that she had to go away and be quiet and remember "just to make it last longer". She felt there'd never be anything as good again for her – so she had to make it last longer.

GERALD *(gravely)*: I see. Well, I never saw her again, and that's all I can tell you.

INSPECTOR: It's all I want to know from you.

GERALD: In that case – as I'm rather more – upset – by this business than I probably appear to be – and – well, I'd like to be alone for a little while – I'd be glad if you'd let me go.

INSPECTOR: Go where? Home?

GERALD: No. I'll just go out – walk about – for a while, if you don't mind. I'll come back.

INSPECTOR: All right, Mr Croft.

SHEILA: But just in case you forget – or decide not to come back, Gerald, I think you'd better take this with you. *(She hands him the ring.)*

How would you have reacted?

GERALD: I see. Well, I was expecting this.

odd strange

SHEILA: I don't dislike you as I did half an hour ago, Gerald. In fact, in some odd way, I rather respect you more than I've ever done before. I knew anyhow you were lying about those months last year when you hardly came near me. I knew there was something fishy about that time. And now at least you've been honest. And I believe what you told us about the way you helped her at first. Just out of pity. And it was my fault really that she was so desperate when you first met her. But this has made a difference. You and I aren't the same people

fishy seeming false, making one doubtful

who sat down to dinner here. We'd have to start all over again, getting to know each other –

BIRLING: Now, Sheila, I'm not defending him. But you must understand that a lot of young men –

SHEILA: Don't interfere, please, Father. Gerald knows what I mean, and you apparently don't.

GERALD: Yes, I know what you mean. But I'm coming back – if I may.

SHEILA: All right.

MRS BIRLING: Well, really, I don't know. I think we've just about come to an end of this wretched business –

GERALD: I don't think so. Excuse me.

He goes out. They watch him go in silence. We hear the front door slam.

SHEILA *(to* INSPECTOR*)*: You know, you never showed him that photograph of her.

INSPECTOR: No. It wasn't necessary. And I thought it better not to.

MRS BIRLING: You have a photograph of this girl?

INSPECTOR: Yes. I think you'd better look at it.

MRS BIRLING: I don't see any particular reason why I should –

INSPECTOR: Probably not. But you'd better look at it.

MRS BIRLING: Very well. *(He produces the photograph and she looks hard at it.)*

INSPECTOR *(taking back the photograph)*: You recognise her?

MRS BIRLING: No. Why should I?

INSPECTOR: Of course she might have changed lately, but I can't believe she could have changed so much.

MRS BIRLING: I don't understand you, Inspector.

INSPECTOR: You mean you don't choose to do, Mrs Birling.

MRS BIRLING *(angrily)*: I meant what I said.

INSPECTOR: You're not telling me the truth.

MRS BIRLING: I beg your pardon!

BIRLING *(angrily, to* INSPECTOR*)*: Look here, I'm not going to have this, Inspector. You'll apologise at once.

INSPECTOR: Apologise for what – doing my duty?

BIRLING: No, for being so offensive about it. I'm a public man –

---

*__to interfere__ *sich einmischen*

*__apparently__ it seems, as it appears

wretched very terrible

*__to slam__ *zuschlagen*

*__probably__ almost certainly

to have here: to accept, permit, tolerate

*__to apologise__ to say one is sorry

INSPECTOR *(massively)*: Public men, Mr Birling, have responsibilities as well as privileges.

BIRLING: Possibly. But you weren't asked to come here to talk to me about my responsibilities.

SHEILA: Let's hope not. Though I'm beginning to wonder.

MRS BIRLING: Does that mean anything, Sheila?

SHEILA: It means that we've no excuse now for putting on airs and that if we've any sense we won't try. Father threw this girl out because she asked for decent wages. I went and pushed her further out, right into the street, just because I was angry and she was pretty. Gerald set her up as his mistress and then dropped her when it suited him. And now you're pretending you don't recognise her from that photograph. I admit I don't know why you should, but I know jolly well you did in fact recognise her, from the way you looked. And if you're not telling the truth, why should the Inspector apologise? And can't you see, both of you, you're making it worse?

She turns away. We hear the front door slam again.

BIRLING: That was the door again.

MRS BIRLING: Gerald must have come back.

INSPECTOR: Unless your son has just gone out.

BIRLING: I'll see.

He goes out quickly. INSPECTOR *turns to* MRS BIRLING.

INSPECTOR: Mrs Birling, you're a member – a prominent member – of the Brumley Women's Charity Organisation, aren't you?

MRS BIRLING *does not reply.*

SHEILA: Go on, Mother. You might as well admit it. *(To* INSPECTOR.*)* Yes, she is. Why?

INSPECTOR *(calmly)*: It's an organisation to which women in distress can appeal for help in various forms. Isn't that so?

MRS BIRLING *(with dignity)*: Yes. We've done a great deal of useful work in helping deserving cases.

INSPECTOR: There was a meeting of the interviewing committee two weeks ago?

---

to put on airs behaviour intended to make people think one is more important than one really is

**to pretend* *vorgeben*

unless if ... not

Women's Charity Organisation group of women helping other members of society
charity *Wohltätigkeit*

***distress** state of suffering
***to appeal** *appellieren, sich wenden*

interviewing committee women find out in interviews if sb deserves financial support

Mrs Birling: I dare say there was.
Inspector: You know very well there was, Mrs Birling. You were in the chair.
Mrs Birling: And if I was, what business is it of yours?
Inspector *(severely)*: Do you want me to tell you – in plain words?

Enter Birling, *looking rather agitated.*

Birling: That must have been Eric.
Mrs Birling *(alarmed)*: Have you been up to his room?
Birling: Yes. And I called out on both landings. It must have been Eric we heard go out then.
Mrs Birling: Silly boy! Where can he have gone to?
Birling: I can't imagine. But he was in one of his excitable queer moods, and even though we don't need him here –
Inspector *(cutting in, sharply)*: We do need him here. And if he's not back soon, I shall have to go and find him.

Birling *and* Mrs Birling *exchange bewildered and rather frightened glances.*

Sheila: He's probably just gone to cool off. He'll be back soon.
Inspector *(severely)*: I hope so.
Mrs Birling: And why should you hope so?
Inspector: I'll explain why when you've answered my questions, Mrs Birling.
Birling: Is there any reason why my wife should answer questions from you, Inspector?
Inspector: Yes, a very good reason. You'll remember that Mr Croft told us – quite truthfully, I believe – that he hadn't spoken to or seen Eva Smith since last September. But Mrs Birling spoke to and saw her only two weeks ago.
Sheila *(astonished)*: Mother!
Birling: Is this true?
Mrs Birling *(after a pause)*: Yes, quite true.
Inspector: She appealed to your organisation for help?
Mrs Birling: Yes.
Inspector: Not as Eva Smith?
Mrs Birling: No. Nor as Daisy Renton.

to be in the chair *den Vorsitz führen*

***severe** critical /

agitated worried

landing *Treppenabsatz*

astounded filled with shocked surprise
gross [grəʊs] stupid
* **impertinence** *Unverschämtheit*
* **to prejudice** to influence
* **impudence** *Frechheit*
stung (to sting) to feel a sharp pain
* **claim** a demand for sth, a right to sth
to bring pressure to bear *Druck ausüben*
* **investigation** careful examination

INSPECTOR: As what then?

MRS BIRLING: First, she called herself Mrs Birling –

BIRLING *(astounded)*: Mrs Birling!

MRS BIRLING: Yes. I think it was simply a piece of gross impertinence – quite deliberate – and naturally that was one of the things that prejudiced me against her case.

BIRLING: And I should think so! Damned impudence!

INSPECTOR: You admit being prejudiced against her case?

MRS BIRLING: Yes.

SHEILA: Mother, she's just died a horrible death – don't forget.

MRS BIRLING: I'm very sorry. But I think she had only herself to blame.

INSPECTOR: Was it owing to your influence, as the most prominent member of the committee, that help was refused the girl?

MRS BIRLING: Possibly.

INSPECTOR: Was it or was it not your influence?

MRS BIRLING *(stung)*: Yes, it was. I didn't like her manner. She'd impertinently made use of our name, though she pretended afterwards it just happened to be the first she thought of. She had to admit, after I began questioning her, that she had no claim to the name, that she wasn't married, and that the story she told at first – about a husband who'd deserted her – was quite false. It didn't take me long to get the truth – or some of the truth – out of her.

INSPECTOR: Why did she want help?

MRS BIRLING: You know very well why she wanted help.

INSPECTOR: No, I don't. I know why she *needed* help. But as I wasn't there, I don't know what she asked from your committee.

MRS BIRLING: I don't think we need discuss it.

INSPECTOR: You have no hope of *not* discussing it, Mrs Birling.

MRS BIRLING: If you think you can bring any pressure to bear upon me, Inspector, you're quite mistaken. Unlike the other three, I did nothing I'm ashamed of or that won't bear investigation. The girl asked for assistance. We are asked to look carefully into the claims made upon us. I wasn't satisfied with this girl's claim – she seemed to me to be not a good case – and so I used my influence to have it refused. And in spite of what's happened to the girl since, I consider I did my duty. So if I prefer not to discuss it any further, you have no power to make me change my mind.

INSPECTOR: Yes I have.

MRS BIRLING: No you haven't. Simply because I've done nothing wrong – and you know it.

INSPECTOR *(very deliberately)*: I think you did something terribly wrong – and that you're going to spend the rest of your life regretting it. I wish you'd been with me tonight in the Infirmary. You'd have seen –

SHEILA *(bursting in)*: No, no, please! Not that again. I've imagined it enough already.

INSPECTOR *(very deliberately)*: Then the next time you imagine it, just remember that this girl was going to have a child.

SHEILA *(horrified)*: No! Oh – horrible – horrible! How could she have wanted to kill herself?

INSPECTOR: Because she'd been turned out and turned down too many times. This was the end.

SHEILA: Mother, you must have known.

INSPECTOR: It was because she was going to have a child that she went for assistance to your mother's committee.

BIRLING: Look here, this wasn't Gerald Croft –

INSPECTOR *(cutting in, sharply)*: No, no. Nothing to do with him.

SHEILA: Thank goodness for that! Though I don't know why I should care now.

INSPECTOR *(to* MRS BIRLING*)*: And you've nothing further to tell me, eh?

MRS BIRLING: I'll tell you what I told her. Go and look for the father of the child. It's his responsibility.

INSPECTOR: That doesn't make it any the less yours. She came to you for help, at a time when no woman could have needed it more. And you not only refused it yourself but saw to it that the others refused it too. She was here alone, friendless, almost penniless, desperate. She needed not only money, but advice, sympathy, friendliness. You've had chil-

deliberate slow, careful unhurried

***to horrify** to shock

goodness for God

to see to to make sure about

***sympathy** *Zuneigung, Mitleid*

- **vile** *gemein*
- ***dubious** feeling uncertain
- **inquest** *gerichtliche Untersuchung*
- **pack** number
- **to compel** to make so do sth by force
- **to give oneself airs** *affektiertes Getue*
- **elaborate** detailed and complicated
- ***scruple** *Bedenken*
- **slab** *Platte, im Leichenschauhaus*
- **to stammer** *stammeln*
- **to yammer** to complain in a sad voice
- **to cow** to make afraid

dren. You must have known what she was feeling. And you slammed the door in her face.

Sheila (*with feeling*): Mother, I think it was cruel and vile.

Birling (*dubiously*): I must say, Sybil, that when this comes out at the inquest, it isn't going to do us much good. The Press might easily take it up –

Mrs Birling (*agitated now*): Oh, stop it, both of you. And please remember before you start accusing me of anything again that it wasn't I who had her turned out of her employment – which probably began it all. (*Turning to* Inspector.) In the circumstances I think I was justified. The girl had begun by telling us a pack of lies. Afterwards, when I got at the truth, I discovered that she knew who the father was, she was quite certain about that, and so I told her it was her business to make him responsible. If he refused to marry her – and in my opinion he ought to be compelled to – then he must at least support her.

Inspector: And what did she reply to that?

Mrs Birling: Oh – a lot of silly nonsense!

Inspector: What was it?

Mrs Birling: Whatever it was, I know it made me finally lose all patience with her. She was giving herself ridiculous airs. She was claiming elaborate fine feelings and scruples that were simply absurd in a girl in her position.

Inspector (*very sternly*): Her position now is that she lies with a burnt-out inside on a slab. (*As* Birling *tries to protest, turns on him.*) Don't stammer and yammer at me again, man. I'm losing all patience with you people. *What did she say?*

Mrs Birling (*rather cowed*): She said that the father was only a youngster – silly and wild and drinking too much. There couldn't be any question of marrying him – it would be wrong for them both. He had given her money but she didn't want to take any more money from him.

Inspector: Why didn't she want to take any more money from him?

Mrs Birling: All a lot of nonsense – I didn't believe a word of it.

Inspector: I'm not asking you if you believed it. I want to know what she said. Why didn't she want to take any more money from this boy?

MRS BIRLING: Oh – she had some fancy reason. As if a girl of that sort would ever refuse money!

INSPECTOR *(sternly)*: I warn you, you're making it worse for yourself. What reason did she give for not taking any more money?

MRS BIRLING: Her story was – that he'd said something one night, when he was drunk, that gave her the idea that it wasn't his money.

INSPECTOR: Where had he got it from then?

MRS BIRLING: He'd stolen it.

INSPECTOR: So she'd come to you for assistance because she didn't want to take stolen money?

MRS BIRLING: That's the story she finally told, after I'd refused to believe her original story – that she was a married woman who'd been deserted by her husband. I didn't see any reason to believe that one story should be any truer than the other. Therefore, you're quite wrong to suppose I shall regret what I did.

INSPECTOR: But if her story was true, if this boy had been giving her stolen money, then she came to you for help because she wanted to keep this youngster out of any more trouble – isn't that so?

MRS BIRLING: Possibly. But it sounded ridiculous to me. So I was perfectly justified in advising my committee not to allow her claim for assistance.

INSPECTOR: You're not even sorry now, when you know what happened to the girl?

MRS BIRLING: I'm sorry she should have come to such a horrible end. But I accept no blame for it at all.

INSPECTOR: Who is to blame then?

MRS BIRLING: First, the girl herself.

SHEILA *(bitterly)*: For letting Father and me have her chucked out of her jobs!

MRS BIRLING: Secondly, I blame the young man who was the father of the child she was going to have. If, as she said, he didn't belong to her class, and was some drunken young idler, then that's all the more reason why he shouldn't escape. He should be made an example of. If the girl's death is due to anybody, then it's due to him.

INSPECTOR: And if her story is true – that he was stealing money –

MRS BIRLING *(rather agitated now)*: There's no point in assuming that –

fancy imaginary

***to regret** to be sorry about

***no blame** no responsibility or guilt

to chuck (coll) to dismiss

idler *Rumtreiber*
to make an example of to punish as a warning to others
due to caused by
point here: sense

***to assume** *annehmen*
assuming *anmaßend*
assumption *Annahme*
assumed *angenommen*

INSPECTOR: But suppose we do, what then?

MRS BIRLING: Then he'd be entirely responsible – because the girl wouldn't have come to us, and have been refused assistance, if it hadn't been for him –

INSPECTOR: So he's the chief culprit anyhow.

***culprit** the person guilty of a crime

MRS BIRLING: Certainly. And he ought to be dealt with very severely –

SHEILA *(with sudden alarm)*: Mother – stop – stop!

BIRLING: Be quiet, Sheila!

SHEILA: But don't you see –

MRS BIRLING *(severely)*: You're behaving like a hysterical child tonight. (*Sheila begins crying quietly. Mrs Birling turns to Inspector.*) And if you'd take some steps to find this young man and then make sure that he's compelled to confess in public his responsibility – instead of staying here asking quite unnecessary questions – then you really would be doing your duty.

INSPECTOR *(grimly)*: Don't worry, Mrs Birling. I shall do my duty. *(He looks at his watch.)*

MRS BIRLING *(triumphantly)*: I'm glad to hear it.

INSPECTOR: No hushing up, eh? Make an example of the young man, eh? Public confession of responsibility – um?

to hush up to keep secret, to prevent the public from knowing about

MRS BIRLING: Certainly. I consider it your duty. And now no doubt you'd like to say good night.

INSPECTOR: Not yet. I'm waiting.

MRS BIRLING: Waiting for what?

INSPECTOR: To do my duty.

SHEILA *(distressed)*: Now, Mother – don't you see?

MRS BIRLING *(understanding now)*: But surely ... I mean ... it's ridiculous ...

She stops, and exchanges a frightened glance with her husband.

BIRLING *(terrified now)*: Look, Inspector, you're not trying to tell us that – that my boy – is mixed up in this –?

***to terrify** to frighten, to fill with terror or fear

INSPECTOR *(sternly)*: If he is, then we know what to do, don't we? Mrs Birling has just told us.

BIRLING *(thunderstruck)*: My God! But – look here –

thunderstruck extremely surprised, shocked

MRS BIRLING *(agitated)*: I don't believe it. I *won't* believe it ...

SHEILA: Mother – I begged you and begged you to stop –

INSPECTOR holds up a hand. We hear the front door. They wait, looking towards door. ERIC enters, looking extremely pale and distressed. He meets their enquiring stares.
Curtain falls quickly.

End of Act Two

Which questions would you like to ask either of the characters?

Act Three

Exactly as at end of Act II. Eric *is standing just inside the room and the others are staring at him.*

Eric: You know, don't you?

Inspector *(as before)*: Yes, we know.

Eric *shuts the door and comes further in.*

Mrs Birling *(distressed)*: Eric, I can't believe it. There must be some mistake. You don't know what we've been saying.

Sheila: It's a good job for him he doesn't, isn't it?

Eric: Why?

Sheila: Because mother's been busy blaming everything on the young man who got this girl into trouble, and saying he shouldn't escape and should be made an example of –

Birling: That's enough, Sheila.

Eric *(bitterly)*: You haven't made it any easier for me, have you, Mother?

Mrs Birling: But I didn't know it was *you* – I never dreamt. Besides, you're not that type – you don't get drunk –

Sheila: Of course he does. I told you he did.

Eric: *You* told her. Why, you little sneak!

sneak (infml) a cowardly deceitful person, esp. one who informs on others

Sheila: No, that's not fair, Eric. I could have told her months ago, but of course I didn't. I only told her tonight because I knew everything was coming out – it was simply bound to come out tonight – so I thought she might as well know in advance. Don't forget – I've already been through it.

Mrs Birling: Sheila, I simply don't understand your attitude.

Birling: Neither do I. If you'd had any sense of loyalty –

Inspector *(cutting in, smoothly)*: Just a minute, Mrs Birling. There'll be plenty of time, when I've gone, for you all to adjust your family relationships. But now I must hear what your son has to tell me. *(Sternly, to the three of them)* And I'll be obliged if

to adjust to put into order

you'll let us get on without any further interruptions. *(Turning to* ERIC.*)* Now then.

ERIC *(miserably)*: Could I have a drink first?

BIRLING *(explosively)*: No.

INSPECTOR *(firmly)*: Yes. *(As* BIRLING *looks like interrupting explosively)* I know – he's your son and this is your house – but look at him. He needs a drink now just to see him through.

BIRLING *(to* ERIC*)*: All right. Go on.

ERIC *goes for a whisky. His whole manner of handling the decanter and then the drink shows his familiarity with quick heavy drinking. The others watch him narrowly.*

(Bitterly) I understand a lot of things now I didn't understand before.

INSPECTOR: Don't start on that. I want to get on. *(To* ERIC.*)* When did you first meet this girl?

ERIC: One night last November.

INSPECTOR: Where did you meet her?

ERIC: In the Palace bar. I'd been there an hour or so with two or three chaps. I was a bit squiffy.

INSPECTOR: What happened then?

ERIC: I began talking to her, and stood her a few drinks. I was rather far gone by the time we had to go.

INSPECTOR: Was she drunk too?

ERIC: She told me afterwards that she was a bit, chiefly because she'd not had much to eat that day.

INSPECTOR: Why had she gone there – ?

ERIC: She wasn't the usual sort. But – well, I suppose she didn't know what to do. There was some woman who wanted her to go there. I never quite understood about that.

INSPECTOR: You went with her to her lodgings that night?

ERIC: Yes, I insisted – it seems. I'm not very clear about it, but afterwards she told me she didn't want me to go in but that – well, I was in that state when a chap easily turns nasty – and I threatened to make a row.

INSPECTOR: So she let you in?

ERIC: And that's when it happened. And I didn't even remember – that's the hellish thing. Oh – my God! – how stupid it all is!

***to be obliged** to be grateful
obligation a duty
obligatory necessary, sth which must be done

to see to help

chap (coll) fellow
squiffy (infml) slightly drunk

to stand to pay for

far gone here: very drunk

row [raʊ] a noisy quarrel

MRS BIRLING *(with a cry)*: Oh – Eric – how could you?

BIRLING *(sharply)*: Sheila, take your mother along to the drawing-room –

SHEILA *(protesting)*: But – I want to –

BIRLING *(very sharply)*: You heard what I said. *(Gentler)* Go on, Sybil.

He goes to open the door while SHEILA *takes her mother out. Then he closes it and comes in.*

INSPECTOR: When did you meet her again?

ERIC: About a fortnight afterwards.

INSPECTOR: By appointment?

ERIC: No. And I couldn't remember her name or where she lived. It was all very vague. But I happened to see her again in the Palace bar.

INSPECTOR: More drinks?

ERIC: Yes, though that time I wasn't so bad.

INSPECTOR: But you took her home again?

ERIC: Yes. And this time we talked a bit. She told me something about herself and I talked too. Told her my name and what I did.

INSPECTOR: And you made love again?

ERIC: Yes. I wasn't in love with her or anything – but I liked her – she was pretty and a good sport –

BIRLING *(harshly)*: So you had to go to bed with her?

ERIC: Well, I'm old enough to be married, aren't I, and I'm not married, and I hate these fat old tarts round the town – the ones I see some of your respectable friends with –

BIRLING *(angrily)*: I don't want any of that talk from you –

INSPECTOR *(very sharply)*: I don't want any of it from either of you. Settle it afterwards. *(To* ERIC.*)* Did you arrange to see each other after that?

ERIC: Yes. And the next time – or the time after that – she told me she thought she was going to have a baby. She wasn't quite sure. And then she was.

INSPECTOR: And of course she was very worried about it?

ERIC: Yes, and so was I. I was in a hell of a state about it.

INSPECTOR: Did she suggest that you ought to marry her?

ERIC: No. She didn't want me to marry her. Said I didn't love her – and all that. In a way, she treated

---

***appointment** agreement of a time and place for a meeting
appointed arranged, settled, fixed
to appoint to put in or choose for a position

sport (infml) person who reacts in a cheerful, pleasant way

tart (sl) prostitute

a hell of a state terrible condition, horrible state

me – as if I were a kid. Though I was nearly as old as she was.

INSPECTOR: So what did you propose to do?

ERIC: Well, she hadn't a job – and didn't feel like trying again for one – and she'd no money left – so I insisted on giving her enough money to keep her going – until she refused to take any more –

INSPECTOR: How much did you give her altogether?

ERIC: I suppose – about fifty pounds all told.

all told in all

BIRLING: Fifty pounds – on top of drinking and going round the town! Where did you get fifty pounds from?

As ERIC *does not reply,*

INSPECTOR: That's my question too.

ERIC *(miserably)*: I got it – from the office –

BIRLING: My office?

ERIC: Yes.

INSPECTOR: You mean – you stole the money?

ERIC: Not really.

BIRLING *(angrily)*: What do you mean – not really?

ERIC *does not reply because now* MRS BIRLING *and* SHEILA *come back.*

SHEILA: This isn't my fault.

MRS BIRLING *(to* BIRLING*)*: I'm sorry, Arthur, but I simply couldn't stay in there. I had to know what's happening.

BIRLING *(savagely)*: Well, I can tell you what's happening. He's admitted he was responsible for the girl's condition, and now he's telling us he supplied her with money he stole from the office.

savage fierce *(grimmig)*

*__to supply__ to provide, to give things to (a person) for use

MRS BIRLING *(shocked)*: Eric! You stole money?

ERIC: No, not really. I intended to pay it back.

BIRLING: We've heard that story before. How could you have paid it back?

ERIC: I'd have managed somehow. I had to have some money –

BIRLING: I don't understand how you could take as much as that out of the office without somebody knowing.

ERIC: There were some small accounts to collect, and I asked for cash –

account here: *Rechnungsbetrag*

BIRLING: Gave the firm's receipt and then kept the money, eh?

*__receipt__ a written statement that one has received money

to cover up to hide a mistake, sth illegal

***mess** *Patsche, Klemme*

***startled** surprised

at breaking point on the point of breaking down, losing control of one's feelings

***to threaten** *bedrohen*
threat sth or sb regarded as a possible danger
threateningly

ERIC: Yes.

BIRLING: You must give me a list of those accounts. I've got to cover this up as soon as I can. You damned fool – why didn't you come to me when you found yourself in this mess?

ERIC: Because you're not the kind of father a chap could go to when he's in trouble – that's why.

BIRLING *(angrily)*: Don't talk to me like that. Your trouble is – you've been spoilt –

INSPECTOR *(cutting in)*: And my trouble is – that I haven't much time. You'll be able to divide the responsibility between you when I've gone. *(To* ERIC.*)* Just one last question, that's all. The girl discovered that this money you were giving her was stolen, didn't she?

ERIC *(miserably)*: Yes. That was the worst of all. She wouldn't take any more, and she didn't want to see me again. *(Sudden startled tone.)* Here, but how did you know that? Did she tell you?

INSPECTOR: No. She told me nothing. I never spoke to her.

SHEILA: She told mother.

MRS BIRLING *(alarmed)*: Sheila!

SHEILA: Well, he has to know.

ERIC: *(to* MRS BIRLING*)*: She told you? Did she come here – but then she couldn't have done, she didn't even know I lived here. What happened? *(*MRS BIRLING, *distressed, shakes her head but does not reply.)* Come on, don't just look like that. Tell me – tell me – what happened?

INSPECTOR *(with calm authority)*: I'll tell you. She went to your mother's committee for help, after she'd done with you. Your mother refused that help.

ERIC *(nearly at breaking point)*: Then – you killed her. She came to you to protect me – and you turned her away – yes, and you killed her – and the child she'd have had too – my child – your own grandchild – you killed them both – damn you, damn you –

MRS BIRLING *(very distressed now)*: No – Eric – please – I didn't know – I didn't understand –

ERIC *(almost threatening her)*: You don't understand anything. You never did. You never even tried – you –

SHEILA *(frightened)*: Eric, don't – don't –

BIRLING *(furious, intervening)*: Why, you hysterical young fool – get back – or I'll –

INSPECTOR *(taking charge, masterfully)*: Stop! *(They are suddenly quiet, staring at him.)* And be quiet for a moment and listen to me. I don't need to know any more. Neither do you. This girl killed herself – and died a horrible death. But each of you helped to kill her. Remember that. Never forget it. *(He looks from one to the other of them carefully.)* But then I don't think you ever will. Remember what you did, Mrs Birling. You turned her away when she most needed help. You refused her even the pitiable little bit of organised charity you had in your power to grant her. Remember what you did –

ERIC *(unhappily)*: My God – I'm not likely to forget.

INSPECTOR: Just used her for the end of a stupid drunken evening, as if she was an animal, a thing, not a person. No, you won't forget. *(He looks at* SHEILA.*)*

SHEILA *(bitterly)*: I know. I had her turned out of a job. I started it.

INSPECTOR: You helped – but didn't start it. *(Rather savagely, to* BIRLING.*)* You started it. She wanted twenty-five shillings a week instead of twenty-two and sixpence. You made her pay a heavy price for that. And now she'll make you pay a heavier price still.

BIRLING *(unhappily)*: Look, Inspector – I'd give thousands – yes, thousands –

INSPECTOR: You're offering the money at the wrong time, Mr Birling. *(He makes a move as if concluding the session, possibly shutting up notebook, etc. Then surveys them sardonically.)* No, I don't think any of you will forget. Nor that young man, Croft, though he at least had some affection for her and made her happy for a time. Well, Eva Smith's gone. You can't do her any more harm. And you can't do her any good now, either. You can't even say "I'm sorry, Eva Smith".

SHEILA *(who is crying quietly)*: That's the worst of it.

INSPECTOR: But just remember this. One Eva Smith has gone – but there are millions and millions and millions of Eva Smiths and John Smiths still left with us, with their lives, their hopes and fears, their suffering, and chance of happiness, all intertwined

****to intervene** to interrupt

∢ How would Mr Birling have finished the sentence if the Inspector had not interrupted him?

pitiable *erbärmlich, kläglich, armselig*

to grant (fml) to give

to survey to look at (a group) as a whole
sardonically cynically, with a bitter laugh

intertwined *verbunden*

anguish very great pain and suffering
***to subdue** to overcome
subdued unnaturally or unusually quiet in behaviour
gloomy sad
stormy showing feelings, passionate
drop that (coll) stop saying that
to turn out to develop, to happen, to result

with our lives, with what we think and say and do. We don't live alone. We are members of one body. We are responsible for each other. And I tell you that the time will soon come when, if men will not learn that lesson, then they will be taught it in fire and blood and anguish. Good night.

He walks straight out, leaving them staring, subdued and wondering. SHEILA *is still quietly crying.* MRS BIRLING *has collapsed into a chair.* ERIC *is brooding desperately.* BIRLING, *the only active one, hears the front door slam, moves hesitatingly towards the door, stops, looks gloomily at the other three, then pours himself out a drink, which he hastily swallows.*

BIRLING *(angrily to* ERIC*)*: You're the one I blame for this.

ERIC: I'll bet I am.

BIRLING *(angrily)*: Yes, and you don't realise yet all you've done. Most of this is bound to come out. There'll be a public scandal.

ERIC: Well, I don't care now.

BIRLING: You! You don't seem to care about anything. But I care. I was almost certain for a knighthood in the next Honours List –

ERIC *laughs rather hysterically, pointing at him.*

ERIC *(laughing)*: Oh – for God's sake! What does it matter now whether they give you a knighthood or not?

BIRLING *(stormily)*: It doesn't matter to you. Apparently nothing matters to you. But it may interest you to know that until every penny of that money you stole is repaid, you'll work for nothing. And there's going to be no more of this drinking round the town – and picking up women in the Palace bar –

MRS BIRLING *(coming to life)*: I should think not. Eric, I'm absolutely ashamed of you.

ERIC: Well, I don't blame you. But don't forget I'm ashamed of you as well – yes, both of you.

BIRLING *(angrily)*: Drop that. There's every excuse for what both your mother and I did – it turned out unfortunately, that's all –

SHEILA *(scornfully)*: That's all.

BIRLING: Well, what have you to say?

SHEILA: I don't know where to begin.

BIRLING: Then don't begin. Nobody wants you to.

SHEILA: I behaved badly too. I know I did. I'm ashamed of it. But now you're beginning all over again to pretend that nothing much has happened –

BIRLING: Nothing much has happened! Haven't I already said there'll be a public scandal – unless we're lucky – and who here will suffer from that more than I will?

SHEILA: But that's not what I'm talking about. I don't care about that. The point is, you don't seem to have learnt anything.

BIRLING: Don't I? Well, you're quite wrong there. I've learnt plenty tonight. And you don't want me to tell you what I've learnt, I hope. When I look back on tonight – when I think of what I was feeling when the five of us sat down to dinner at that table –

ERIC *(cutting in)*: Yes, and do you remember what you said to Gerald and me after dinner, when you were feeling so pleased with yourself? You told us that a man has to make his own way, look after himself and mind his own business, and that we weren't to take any notice of these cranks who tell us that everybody has to look after everybody else, as if we were all mixed up together. Do you remember? Yes – and then one of those cranks walked in – the Inspector. *(Laughs bitterly.)* I didn't notice you told him that it's every man for himself.

SHEILA *(sharply attentive)*: Is that when the Inspector came, just after Father had said that?

ERIC: Yes. What of it?

MRS BIRLING: Now what's the matter, Sheila?

SHEILA *(slowly)*: It's queer – very queer – *(She looks at them reflectively.)*

MRS BIRLING *(with some excitement)*: I know what you're going to say. Because I've been wondering myself.

SHEILA: It doesn't much matter now, of course – but was he really a police inspector?

BIRLING: Well, if he wasn't, it matters a devil of a lot. Makes all the difference.

SHEILA: No, it doesn't.

scornfully *verächtlich*

***attentive** taking careful notice; listening carefully

What of it? Why is that important?

queer strange

***reflective** thoughtful
to reflect on to consider carefully
to reflect to throw back (heat, light, sound, or an image)
reflection

a devil of a lot (coll) very much

BIRLING: Don't talk rubbish. Of course it does.

oughtn't shouldn't

SHEILA: Well, it doesn't to me. And it oughtn't to you, either.

MRS BIRLING: Don't be childish, Sheila.

to flare up to become suddenly angry

SHEILA *(flaring up)*: I'm not being. If you want to know, it's you two who are being childish – trying not to face the facts.

BIRLING: I won't have that sort of talk. Any more of that and you leave this room.

ERIC: That'll be terrible for her, won't it?

SHEILA: I'm going anyhow in a minute or two. But don't you see, if all that's come out tonight is true, then it doesn't much matter who it was who made us confess. And it was true, wasn't it? You turned the girl out of one job, and I had her turned out of another. Gerald kept her – at a time when he was supposed to be too busy to see me. Eric – well, we know what Eric did. And Mother hardened her heart and gave her the final push that finished her. That's what's important – and not whether a man is a police inspector or not.

What is implied in the statement? ➤

ERIC: He was our police inspector all right.

SHEILA: That's what I mean, Eric. But if it's any comfort to you – and it isn't to me – I have an idea – and I had it all along vaguely – that there was something curious about him. He never seemed like an ordinary police inspector –

BIRLING *(rather excited)*: You're right. I felt it too. *(To* MRS BIRLING.*)* Didn't you?

MRS BIRLING: Well, I must say his manner was quite extraordinary; so – so rude – and assertive –

assertive here: *anmaßend*

BIRLING: Then look at the way he talked to me. Telling me to shut up – and so on. He must have known I was an ex-Lord Mayor and a magistrate and so forth. Besides – the way he talked – you remember. I mean, they don't *talk* like that. I've had dealings with dozens of them.

SHEILA: All right. But it doesn't make any real difference, y'know.

MRS BIRLING: Of course it does.

ERIC: No, Sheila's right. It doesn't.

BIRLING *(angrily)*: That's comic, that is, coming from you. You're the one it makes *most* difference to. You've confessed to theft, and now he knows all

*__theft__ stealing

about it, and he can bring it out at the inquest, and then if necessary carry it to court. He can't do anything to your mother and Sheila and me – except perhaps make us look a bit ashamed of ourselves in public – but as for you, he can ruin you. You know.

SHEILA *(slowly)*: We hardly ever told him anything he didn't know. Did you notice that?

BIRLING: That's nothing. He had a bit of information, left by the girl, and made a few smart guesses – but the fact remains that if we hadn't talked so much, he'd have had little to go on. *(Looks angrily at them.)* And really, when I come to think of it, why you all had to go letting everything come out like that, beats me.

SHEILA: It's all right talking like that now. But he made us confess.

MRS BIRLING: He certainly didn't make me *confess* – as you call it. I told him quite plainly that I thought I had done no more than my duty.

SHEILA: Oh – Mother!

BIRLING: The fact is, you allowed yourselves to be bluffed. Yes – bluffed.

MRS BIRLING *(protesting)*: Now really – Arthur.

BIRLING: No, not you, my dear. But these two. That fellow obviously didn't like us. He was prejudiced from the start. Probably a Socialist or some sort of crank – he talked like one. And then, instead of standing up to him, you let him bluff you into talking about your private affairs. You ought to have stood up to him.

ERIC *(sulkily)*: Well, I didn't notice you standing up to him.

BIRLING: No, because by that time you'd admitted you'd been taking money. What chance had I after that? I was a fool not to have insisted upon seeing him alone.

ERIC: That wouldn't have worked.

SHEILA: Of course it wouldn't.

MRS BIRLING: Really, from the way you children talk, you might be wanting to help him instead of us. Now just be quiet so that your father can decide what we ought to do. *(Looks expectantly at* BIRLING.*)*

*__smart__ clever
*__guess__ *Vermutung, Annahme*

__it beats me__ I don't know why

*__prejudiced__ *voreingenommen*

__crank__ *Wirrkopf*
__to stand up to__ to meet bravely

__sulky__ miserable and unfriendly

to wait up not to go to bed

* **relieved** *erleichtert*

to withdraw to move away or back

BIRLING *(dubiously)*: Yes – well. We'll have to do something – and get to work quickly too. *(As he hesitates there is a ring at the front door. They look at each other in alarm.)* Now who's this? Had I better go?

MRS BIRLING: No. Edna'll go. I asked her to wait up to make us some tea.

SHEILA: It might be Gerald coming back.

BIRLING *(relieved)*: Yes, of course. I'd forgotten about him.

EDNA *appears.*

EDNA: It's Mr Croft.

GERALD *appears, and* EDNA *withdraws.*

GERALD: I hope you don't mind my coming back?

MRS BIRLING: No, of course not, Gerald.

GERALD: I had a special reason for coming. When did that Inspector go?

SHEILA: Only a few minutes ago. He put us all through it –

MRS BIRLING *(warningly)*: Sheila!

SHEILA: Gerald might as well know.

BIRLING *(hastily)*: Now – now – we needn't bother him with all that stuff.

SHEILA: All right. *(To* GERALD.*)* But we're all in it – up to the neck. It got worse after you left.

GERALD: How did he behave?

SHEILA: He was – frightening.

BIRLING: If you ask me, he behaved in a very peculiar and suspicious manner.

MRS BIRLING: The rude way he spoke to Mr Birling and me – it was quite extraordinary!

GERALD: Hm – hm!

They all look enquiringly at GERALD.

BIRLING *(excitedly)*: You know something. What is it?

GERALD *(slowly)*: That man wasn't a police officer.

BIRLING *(astounded)*: What?

MRS BIRLING: Are you certain?

GERALD: I'm almost certain. That's what I came back to tell you.

BIRLING *(excitedly)*: Good lad! You asked about him, eh?

GERALD: Yes. I met a police sergeant I know down the road. I asked him about this Inspector Goole and described the chap carefully to him. He swore there wasn't any Inspector Goole or anybody like him on the force here.

BIRLING: You didn't tell him –

GERALD *(cutting in)*: No, no. I passed it off by saying I'd been having an argument with somebody. But the point is – this sergeant was dead certain they hadn't any inspector at all like the chap who came here.

BIRLING *(excitedly)*: By Jingo! A fake!

MRS BIRLING *(triumphantly)*: Didn't I tell you? Didn't I say I couldn't imagine a real police inspector talking like that to us?

GERALD: Well, you were right. There isn't any such inspector. We've been had.

BIRLING *(beginning to move)*: I'm going to make certain of this.

MRS BIRLING: What are you going to do?

BIRLING: Ring up the Chief Constable – Colonel Roberts.

MRS BIRLING: Careful what you say, dear.

BIRLING *(now at telephone)*: Of course. *(At telephone.)* Brumley eight seven five two. *(To others as he waits.)* I was going to do this anyhow. I've had my suspicions all along. *(At telephone.)* Colonel Roberts, please. Mr Arthur Birling here ... Oh, Roberts – Birling here. Sorry to ring you up so late, but can you tell me if an Inspector Goole has joined your staff lately ... Goole. G–O–O–L–E ... a new man ... tall, clean-shaven. *(Here he can describe the appearance of the actor playing the* INSPECTOR.*)* I see ... yes ... well, that settles it. ... Good night. *(He puts down the telephone and looks at the others.)* There's no Inspector Goole on the police. That man definitely wasn't a police inspector at all. As Gerald says – we've been had.

MRS BIRLING: I felt it all the time. He never talked like one. He never even looked like one.

BIRLING: This makes a difference, y'know. In fact, it makes all the difference.

GERALD: Of course!

---

the force (Brit) *die Polizei*

to pass off to direct attention away from

By Jingo! (an expression of eagerness): You 're 100 % right, by Jingo!
*__fake__ a person who tries to deceive others by pretending to be what he or she is not

had cheated, deceived

all along all the time

staff group of officers

SHEILA *(bitterly)*: I suppose we're all nice people now.

BIRLING: If you've nothing more sensible than that to say, Sheila, you'd better keep quiet.

ERIC: She's right, though.

BIRLING *(angrily)*: And *you*'d better keep quiet anyhow. If that had been a police inspector and he'd heard you confess –

MRS BIRLING *(warningly)*: Arthur – careful!

BIRLING *(hastily)*: Yes, yes.

SHEILA: You see, Gerald, you haven't to know the rest of our crimes and idiocies.

idiocy *Laster*

GERALD: That's all right, I don't want to. *(To* BIRLING.*)* What do you make of this business now? Was it a hoax?

What do you make of? How do you explain?
hoax trick
to put up to to give (sb) the idea of, to suggest sth to sb

BIRLING: Of course. Somebody put that fellow up to coming here and hoaxing us. There are people in this town who dislike me enough to do that. We ought to have seen through it from the first. In the ordinary way, I believe I would have done. But coming like that, bang on top of our little celebration, just when we were all feeling so pleased with ourselves, naturally it took me by surprise.

bang on top of (infml) suddenly in addition to, right into

MRS BIRLING: I wish I'd been here when that man first arrived. I'd have asked *him* a few questions before I allowed him to ask us any.

SHEILA: It's all right saying that now.

MRS BIRLING: I was the only one for you who didn't give in to him. And now I say we must discuss this business quietly and sensibly and decide if there's anything to be done about it.

BIRLING *(with hearty approval)*: You're absolutely right, my dear. Already we've discovered one important fact – that that fellow was a fraud and we've been hoaxed – and that may not be the end of it by any means.

***approval** *Zustimmung*

fraud [ɔː] (derog) a person who pretends to be what he is not

by any means not at all

GERALD: I'm sure it isn't.

BIRLING *(keenly interested)*: You are, eh? Good! *(To* ERIC, *who is restless.)* Eric, sit down.

ERIC *(sulkily)*: I'm all right.

BIRLING: All right? You're anything but all right. And you needn't stand there – as if – as if –

ERIC: As if – what?

BIRLING: As if you'd nothing to do with us. Just remember your own position, young man. If anybody's up to the neck in this business, you are, so you'd better take some interest in it.

ERIC: I do take some interest in it. I take too much, that's my trouble.

SHEILA: It's mine too.

BIRLING: Now listen, you two. If you're still feeling on edge, then the least you can do is to keep quiet. Leave this to us. I'll admit that fellow's antics rattled us a bit. But we've found him out – and all we have to do is to keep our heads. Now it's our turn.

SHEILA: Our turn to do – what?

MRS BIRLING *(sharply)*: To behave sensibly, Sheila – which is more than you're doing.

ERIC *(bursting out)*: What's the use of talking about behaving sensibly? You're beginning to pretend now that nothing's really happened at all. And I can't see it like that. This girl's still dead, isn't she? Nobody's brought her to life, have they?

SHEILA *(eagerly)*: That's just what I feel, Eric. And it's what they don't seem to understand.

ERIC: Whoever that chap was, the fact remains that I did what I did. And Mother did what she did. And the rest of you did what you did to her. It's still the same rotten story whether it's been told to a police inspector or to somebody else. According to you, I ought to feel a lot better – *(To* GERALD.*)* I stole some money, Gerald, you might as well know – *(As* BIRLING *tries to interrupt)* I don't care, let him know. The money's not the important thing. It's what happened to the girl and what we all did to her that matters. And I still feel the same about it, and that's why I don't feel like sitting down and having a nice cosy talk.

SHEILA: And Eric's absolutely right. And it's the best thing any one of us has said tonight and it makes me feel a bit less ashamed of us. You're just beginning to pretend all over again.

BIRLING: Look – for God's sake!

MRS BIRLING *(protesting)*: Arthur!

BIRLING: Well, my dear, they're so damned exasperating. They just won't try to understand our position or to see the difference between a lot of stuff like this coming out in private and a downright public scandal.

on edge (coll) nervous

antics (pl) *(tolle) Streiche*

to rattle (infml) to confuse, to worry

***sensible** reasonable

rotten very bad, very impleasant

to exasperate [ɪɡˈzæspəreɪt] *ärgern, wütend machen*

downright complete

to glare to look in an angry way

to not give a damn not to care at all

account here: explanation

to dodge (infml) to avoid by a trick or in some dishonest way: tax-dodging

evidence proof

artful cleverly deceitful; full of tricks, cunning

ERIC *(shouting)*: And I say the girl's dead and we all helped to kill her – and that's what matters –

BIRLING *(also shouting, threatening* ERIC*)*: And I say – either stop shouting or get out. *(Glaring at him but in quiet tone)* Some fathers I know would have kicked you out of the house anyhow by this time. So hold your tongue if you want to stay here.

ERIC *(quietly, bitterly)*: I don't give a damn now whether I stay here or not.

BIRLING: You'll stay here long enough to give me an account of that money you stole – yes, and to pay it back too.

SHEILA: But that won't bring Eva Smith back to life, will it?

ERIC: And it doesn't alter the fact that we all helped to kill her.

GERALD: But is it a fact?

ERIC: Of course it is. You don't know the whole story yet.

SHEILA: I suppose you're going to prove now you didn't spend last summer keeping this girl instead of seeing me, eh?

GERALD: I did keep a girl last summer. I've admitted it. And I'm sorry, Sheila.

SHEILA: Well, I must admit you came out of it better than the rest of us. The Inspector said that.

BIRLING *(angrily)*: He wasn't an Inspector.

SHEILA *(flaring up)*: Well, he inspected us all right. And don't let's start dodging and pretending now. Between us we drove that girl to commit suicide.

GERALD: Did we? Who says so? Because I say – there's no more real evidence we did than there was that that chap was a police inspector.

SHEILA: Of course there is.

GERALD: No, there isn't. Look at it. A man comes here pretending to be a police officer. It's a hoax of some kind. Now what does he do? Very artfully, working on bits of information he's picked up here and there, he bluffs us into confessing that we've all been mixed up in this girl's life in one way or another.

ERIC: And so we have.

GERALD: But how do you know it's the same girl?

BIRLING *(eagerly)*: Now wait a minute! Let's see how that would work. Now – *(hesitates)* no, it wouldn't.

ERIC: We all admitted it.

GERALD: All right, you all admitted you had something to do with a girl. But how do you know it's the same girl?

He looks round triumphantly at them. As they puzzle this out, he turns to BIRLING, *after pause.*

Look here, Mr Birling. You sack a girl called Eva Smith. You've forgotten, but he shows you a photograph of her and then you remember. Right?

BIRLING: Yes, that part's straightforward enough. But what then?

GERALD: Well, then he happens to know that Sheila once had a girl sacked from Milwards shop. He tells us that it's this same Eva Smith. And he shows her a photograph that she recognises.

SHEILA: Yes. The same photograph.

GERALD: How do you know it's the same photograph? Did you see the one your father looked at?

SHEILA: No, I didn't.

GERALD: And did your father see the one he showed you?

SHEILA: No, he didn't. And I see what you mean now.

GERALD: We've no proof it was the same photograph and therefore no proof it was the same girl. Now take me. I never saw a photograph, remember. He caught me out by suddenly announcing that this girl changed her name to Daisy Renton. I gave myself away at once because I'd known a Daisy Renton.

BIRLING *(eagerly)*: And there wasn't the slightest proof that this Daisy Renton was really Eva Smith. We've only his word for it, and we'd his word for it that he was a police inspector, and we know now he was lying. So he could have been lying all the time.

GERALD: Of course he could. Probably was. Now what happened after I left?

MRS BIRLING: I was upset because Eric had left the house, and this man said that if Eric didn't come back, he'd have to go and find him. Well, that made me feel worse still. And his manner was so severe and he seemed so confident. Then quite suddenly he said I'd seen Eva Smith only two weeks ago.

BIRLING: Those were his exact words.

MRS BIRLING: And like a fool I said Yes I had.

BIRLING: I don't see now why you did that. She didn't call herself Eva Smith when she came to see you at the committee, did she?

MRS BIRLING: No, of course she didn't. But, feeling so worried, when he suddenly turned on me with those questions, I answered more or less as he wanted me to answer.

SHEILA: But, Mother, don't forget that he showed you a photograph of the girl before that, and you obviously recognised it.

GERALD: Did anybody else see it?

MRS BIRLING: No, he showed it only to me.

Do Gerald's explanations sound convincing to you? – Why or why not?

GERALD: Then, don't you see, there's still no proof it was really the same girl. He might have showed you the photograph of any girl who applied to the committee. And how do we know she was really Eva Smith or Daisy Renton?

dead (infml) completely

BIRLING: Gerald's dead right. He could have used a different photograph each time and we'd be none the wiser. We may all have been recognising different girls.

GERALD: Exactly. Did he ask you to identify a photograph, Eric?

ERIC: No. He didn't need a photograph by the time he'd got round to me. But obviously it must have been the girl I knew who went round to see Mother.

GERALD: Why must it?

ERIC: She said she had to have help because she wouldn't take any more stolen money. And the girl I knew had told me that already.

GERALD: Even then, that may have been all nonsense.

you lot (coll) you other people

to do sb in (sl) to kill

ERIC: I don't see much nonsense about it when a girl goes and kills herself. You lot may be letting yourselves out nicely, but I can't. Nor can Mother. We did her in all right.

a put-up job (infml) sth dishonestly arranged in advance in order to trick sb

BIRLING *(eagerly)*: Wait a minute, wait a minute! Don't be in such a hurry to put yourself into court. That interview with your mother could have been just as much a put-up job, like all this police inspector business. The whole damned thing can have been a piece of bluff.

ERIC *(angrily)*: How can it? The girl's dead, isn't she?

GERALD: What girl? There were probably four or five different girls.

ERIC: That doesn't matter to me. The one I knew is dead.

BIRLING: Is she? *How do we know she is?*

GERALD: That's right. You've got it. How do we know any girl killed herself today?

BIRLING *(looking at them all, triumphantly)*: Now answer that one. Let's look at it from this fellow's point of view. We're having a little celebration here and feeling rather pleased with ourselves. Now he has to work a trick on us. Well, the first thing he has to do is to give us such a shock that after that he can bluff us all the time. So he starts right off. A girl has just died in the Infirmary. She drank some strong disinfectant. Died in agony –

ERIC: All right, don't pile it on.

BIRLING *(triumphantly)*: There you are, you see. Just repeating it shakes you a bit. And that's what he had to do. Shake us at once – and then start questioning us – until we didn't know where we were. Oh – let's admit that. He had the laugh of us all right.

to have the laugh of to be able to laught at

ERIC: He could laugh his head off – if I knew it really was all a hoax.

BIRLING: I'm convinced it is. No police enquiry. No one girl that all this happens to. No scandal –

SHEILA: And no suicide?

GERALD *(decisively)*: We can settle that at once.

SHEILA: How?

GERALD: By ringing up the Infirmary. Either there's a dead girl there or there isn't.

BIRLING *(uneasily)*: It will look a bit queer, won't it – ringing up at this time of night –

GERALD: I don't mind doing it.

MRS BIRLING *(emphatically)*: And if there isn't –

*__emphatically__ in a manner that shows emphasis

GERALD: Anyway we'll see. *(He goes to telephone and looks up number. The others watch tensely.)* Brumley eight nine eight six. ... Is that the Infirmary? This is Mr Gerald Croft – of Crofts Limited . ... Yes. ... We're rather worried about one of our employees. Have you had a girl brought in this afternoon who committed suicide by drinking disinfectant – or any like suicide? Yes, I'll wait.

*__tense__ showing nervous anxiety

As he waits, the others show their nervous tension. BIRLING *wipes his brow,* SHEILA *shivers,* ERIC *clasps and unclasps his hand, etc.*

*__to shiver__ to tremble

to clasp to press tightly together

Yes? ... You're certain of that. ... I see. Well, thank you very much. ... Good night. *(He puts down telephone and looks at them.)* No girl has died in there today. Nobody's been brought in after drinking disinfectant. They haven't had a suicide for months.

BIRLING *(triumphantly)*: There you are! Proof positive. The whole story's just a lot of moonshine. Nothing but an elaborate sell! *(He produces a huge sigh of relief.)* Nobody likes to be sold as badly as that – but – for all that – *(He smiles at them all.)* Gerald, have a drink.

moonshine (infml) talk, opinions, etc., that are not based on reality
elaborate sell (infml) carefully prepared deception
for all that in spite of all that

GERALD *(smiling)*: Thanks, I think I could just do with one now.

BIRLING *(going to sideboard)*: So could I.

MRS BIRLING *(smiling)*: And I must say, Gerald, you've argued this very cleverly, and I'm most grateful.

GERALD *(going for his drink)*: Well, you see, while I was out of the house I'd time to cool off and think things out a little.

BIRLING *(giving him a drink)*: Yes, he didn't keep you on the run as he did the rest of us. I'll admit now he gave me a bit of a scare at the time. But I'd a special reason for not wanting any public scandal just now. *(Has his drink now, and raises his glass.)* Well, here's to us. Come on, Sheila, don't look like that. All over now.

to keep sb on the run to keep sb busy
***scare** sudden feeling of fear

here's to us (said when drinking) a toast

SHEILA: The worst part is. But you're forgetting one thing I still can't forget. Everything we said had happened, really had happened. If it didn't end tragically, then that's lucky for us. But it might have done.

BIRLING *(jovially)*: But the whole thing's different now. Come, come, you can see that, can't you? *(Imitating* INSPECTOR *in his final speech.) You all helped to kill her. (Pointing at* SHEILA *and* ERIC, *and laughing.)* And I wish you could have seen the look on your faces when he said that. *(*SHEILA *moves towards door.)* Going to bed, young woman?

jovial (esp of fat old men) full of good humour

SHEILA *(tensely)*: I want to get out of this. It frightens me the way you talk.

BIRLING *(heartily)*: Nonsense! You'll have a good laugh over it yet. Look, you'd better ask Gerald for that ring you gave back to him, hadn't you? Then you'll feel better.

SHEILA *(passionately)*: You're pretending everything's just as it was before.

ERIC: I'm not!

SHEILA: No, but these others are.

BIRLING: Well, isn't it? We've been had, that's all.

SHEILA: So nothing really happened. So there's nothing to be sorry for, nothing to learn. We can all go on behaving just as we did.

MRS BIRLING: Well, why shouldn't we?

SHEILA: I tell you – whoever that Inspector was, it was anything but a joke. You knew it then. You began to learn something. And now you've stopped. You're ready to go on in the same old way.

BIRLING *(amused)*: And you're not, eh?

SHEILA: No, because I remember what he said, how he looked, and what he made me feel. Fire and blood and anguish. And it frightens me the way you talk, and I can't listen to any more of it.

ERIC: And I agree with Sheila. It frightens me too.

BIRLING: Well, go to bed then, and don't stand there being hysterical.

MRS BIRLING: They're over-tired. In the morning they'll be as amused as we are.

GERALD: Everything's all right now, Sheila. *(Holds up the ring.)* What about this ring?

SHEILA: No, not yet. It's too soon. I must think.

➤ Would you accept it? – Why or why not?

BIRLING *(pointing to* ERIC *and* SHEILA*)*: Now look at the pair of them – the famous younger generation who know it all. And they can't even take a joke –

The telephone rings sharply. There is a moment's complete silence. BIRLING *goes to answer it.*

Yes? ... Mr Birling speaking. ... *What?* – Here –

But obviously the other person has rung off. He puts the telephone down slowly and looks in a panic-stricken fashion at the others.

panic-stricken filled with wild terror

BIRLING: That was the police. A girl has just died – on her way to the Infirmary – after swallowing some disinfectant. And a police inspector is on his way here – to ask some – questions –

dumbfounded *verblüfft, sprachlos*

As they stare guiltily and dumbfounded, the curtain falls.

End of Play

The Author

John Boynton Priestley (1894 – 1984) was born in Bradford (Yorkshire) on September 13, 1894. His mother died in the same year and his father, who was a teacher, married again four years later.
Priestley decided to leave school at the age of sixteen, as he wanted to become a writer. To earn a living he worked for a local wool company. His physical work, the people he met and particularly his father's socialist friends influenced him a lot.
When the First World War (1914 – 1918) broke out Priestley joined the infantry at the age of twenty. He hated the war but fought in France and was lucky that he was not killed, because once a German shell exploded only a few yards away, and once he was the victim of a gas attack. After the war Priestley was awarded an ex-officer's grant, and he successfully studied for a degree at Trinity Hall, Cambridge. He took honours in English literature, modern history and political science.
Nevertheless, he thought academic life did not suit him. That is why in 1921 he settled in London with his wife, who died of cancer in 1925. For some time Priestley looked after his two-year-old daughter alone. After remarrying in 1926 he could fully concentrate on his job as a writer again and in the following years he not only became very successful as an essayist, a journalist, and a novelist but also gained a reputation as a serious critic. In London he also began to mix in the same literary circles as George Bernard Shaw, H.G. Wells and Arnold Bennett. In 1932, when he was 38 years old, he wrote his first play, *Dangerous Corner*. It was an instant success, and after this Priestley wrote for the theatre regularly. He wrote about thirty plays, ran his own producing companies and directed two London theatres.
When the Second World War started in 1939, Priestley was deeply moved and terribly shocked by the suffering of millions of people and the brutality of the war. In 1940 during the low point of the war for Britain, his radio

broadcasts touched a national nerve. Similarly, in his writing he developed a strong sense of what the public might respond to. After World War II he was chosen as a delegate of UNESCO and supported groups and organizations that worked for nuclear disarmament.
In 1952 he got divorced from his second wife with whom he had two daughters and a son. Priestley married for a third time in 1953 and lived near Stratford-upon-Avon for many years. Having been influenced by his father's socialist ideas, Priestley remained politically active throughout his life. He was later not only honoured by several universities but in 1977 the Queen also made him a member of the Order of Merit. During his career he published over 120 books, some of which confirmed his reputation as an important writer of the 20th century. Priestley died at the age of eighty-nine on August 14, 1984.

The Ten Commandments

What young people think of the Ten Commandments.

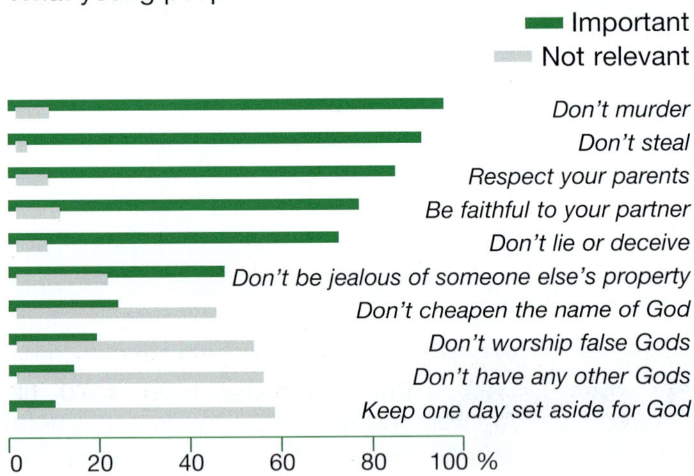

(From "Thou Shalt Not Steal, Except if Poor", The Observer, October 9, 1994)

1. The Ten Commandments demand ethical and moral values. Which of them are relevant for you today?
2. Make inquiries in your course / class to find out about the degree of acceptance. Draw a bar chart to show the distribution of percentages.

3. Compare your findings with the results of the opinion poll that were published in *The Observer* in October 1994.

4. Which values or standards of value do the different characters of the play favour? Refer to
   a) the old Birlings
   b) the young people
   c) the Inspector.

5. How do the value systems of different social classes differ from one another?

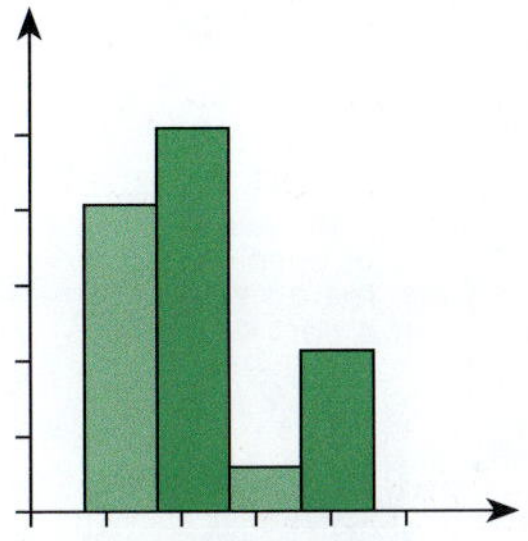

Bar chart

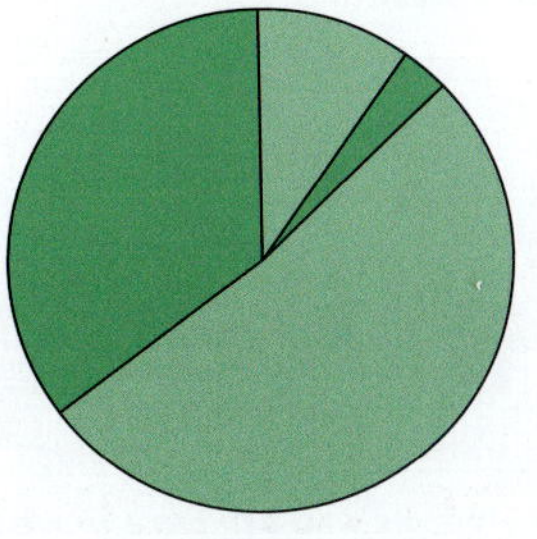

Pie chart

The End of April Posy Simmonds

The woman presented in the cartoon (see next page) looks back on 10 years of the Thatcher government's influence on British society.

Margaret Thatcher was British Prime Minister from 1979 till 1990.

Margaret Thatcher

The end of April

[2] **'cos** (infml) because – [3] **to go on about** to talk about sth for a long time – **ghastly** (infml) very bad – **hunkydory** (infml) fine – [4] **a jolly sight** (infml) very much – [5] **grotty** (sl) bad, unpleasant – **prosciutto** Italian ham – [6] **dump** (sl) a dirty and untidy place – [7] **whirly-eyed** unsteadily moving eyes – **dosser** (Brit sl) a person without a home who sleeps in the open or in cheap lodgings – **to pee** (sl) to urinate – **viburnum** *Schneeballbusch* – [11] **basement** rooms in a house below street level –

[14] **buzz** (infml) a feeling of pleasure or excitement – [15] **mint** (infml) a large amount of money – **cop shop** (sl) police station – **Fort Knox** a particularly safe place where the U.S. federal reserves in gold are kept – [16] **to kit up sb with** to supply sb with necessary things – **thingy** (infml) thing whose name one does not know – **boon** a comfort, a help – **bore** sth which is rather unpleasant – **old bag** (infml derog) unpleasant woman – [18] **pig prod** instrument to make pigs move – **chum** (infml) a good friend – **arse** (sl) bottom – [22] **screecher** instrument making a very shrill sound

1. Describe in your own words what, in the woman's view, has changed for the better.
2. What is her "caring" (picture 11) attitude like?
3. Compare her feeling of responsibility with that of Mr Birling.
4. Write a letter to the woman in which you try to make clear to her that one should treat homeless and old people differently.
5. What is the cartoonist's message? – State whether she successfully conveys it to the reader.
6. Discuss if tolerance and helpfulness are still common values of people in society. Try to refer to as many topical examples as possible to either prove or disprove a particular opinion.

Drama: Useful Words and Phrases

atmosphere
- mood or feeling created by various factors such as scenery, lighting and sound effects, behaviour, tone of voice and diction of characters, etc.

climax
- is reached when a conflict is at its highest point of tension, it often marks the turning-point of the action

drama / play
- literary work meant to be performed on stage
- divided into acts and scenes

dramatic irony
- audience understand implication and meaning of statement but character does not

ending
- can be happy / tragic / surprising

exposition
- gives / provides information on the main characters, time and place of action
- consists of / encompasses the first act / scenes
- arouses reader's / audience's curiosity and interest

falling action
- tension begins to decrease
- conflict is / cannot be solved

foreshadowing
- any hints or clues that indicate what will happen later

irony
- use of words which are clearly the opposite of what one means
- usually either to be amusing or to show annoyance

plot
- series of events causally linked
- there may be a single line of action / a main plot and a sub plot

props
- short for "stage properties" (e. g. pieces of furniture) used on stage

rising action

- develops the conflict
- leads to the climax
- tension / suspense is created (foreshadowing)

scene

- subdivision of play, usually marked by change of place, entry or exit of character
- traditionally: subdivision of act

setting

- time and place of action
- social background / class
- scenery and properties (props) may be important to create a particular atmosphere or mood

stage directions

- notes added to the script of a play
- indicate character's appearance, manner, style of delivery, performance, gestures and movements, details of location, scenery and effects

suspense

- state of curiosity, excitement and anxiety which the reader / audience experiences about the outcome of a situation

How to Write a Characterization

1. Mark / collect all the information that is given on a character.
2. Introduce the character and the situation he / she is in. Refer to his / her social background / position / job / role in the family.
3. Start characterizing her/him directly, i. e. name age/ describe outward appearance / consider what is said directly about the person (stage directions).
4. Refer to the traits of character that are revealed indirectly. Consider what a character does, how he / she reacts or behaves, what persons think and feel, the mood they are in, how they respond to others.
5. Try to sum up if a character develops / changes in the course of events (complex / round) or if he / she does not change his / her attitude (flat character).

Characterization: Useful Words and Phrases

✔ Are there any additional words and phrases?

Mr / Mrs ... is a man / woman in his / her fifties / thirties / ...
He / She ... is presented / described as ...
It is said that he / she looks / seems to be ...
On the one hand he / she is portrayed / depicted as a person who ...
On the other hand he / she ...
It is characteristic of / typical of him / her that ...
He / she is also characterized by his / her attitude towards ... / reaction to ...
which is revealed / underlined by his / her words / reactions / gestures / facial expressions
He / she behaves arrogantly / pretends to be superior when ...
He / she speaks in a low / loud voice / shouts at ...
He / she shows emotions / feelings / that he / she is moved / nervous
excited / irritated
He / she seems to feel insecure / be convinced of himself / be in a bad / good mood
as / when he / she refers to / answers ...
This idea is revealed when he / she says that "..." (l. ...)
He / she is aware of the fact that ...
His / her behaviour shows that he / she is curious / jealous / frightened / taken by surprise / self-confident / convinced that ... / interested in ...
His / her way of treating ... is harsh / friendly / gentle / arrogant / patronizing / contemptuous
He / she creates the impression that he / she is a man / woman who ...
An essential component of his / her character is ...
The reader / audience may conclude from his / her behaviour that ...
During the evening / play / in the course of action he / she undergoes a development /
remains essentially unchanged
The character changes his / her attitude towards ...
He / she is a flat / complex (round) character / an individual and not just mere type
One can easily identify with ... / you feel pity / sympathize with / dislike him / her because ...